Draft Communications Data Bill

Presented to Parliament
by the Secretary of State for the Home Department
by Command of Her Majesty

June 2012

Cm 8359

CONTENTS

FOREWORD BY THE HOME SECRETARY

 Communications technologies and services are changing fast. More communications are taking place on the internet using a wider range of services. As criminals make increasing use of internet based communications, we need to ensure that the police and intelligence agencies continue to have the tools they need to do the job we ask of them: investigating crime and terrorism, protecting the vulnerable and bringing criminals to justice.

For many years our police and security and intelligence agencies have used communications data from landline telephones and mobiles to catch criminals and to protect the public. This information – which does not include the content of a phone call or email – has played a role in nearly every serious organised crime investigation and in all major Security Service counter-terrorism operations over the past decade and is fundamental to policing across the UK. But the ability of the police and others to use this vital tool is disappearing because communications data from new technologies is less available and often harder to access. Without action there is a serious and growing risk that crimes enabled by email and the internet will go undetected and unpunished, that the vulnerable will not be protected and that terrorists and criminals will not be caught and prosecuted. No responsible Government could allow such a situation to develop unaddressed.

The purpose of this Bill, therefore, is to protect the public and bring offenders to justice by ensuring that communications data is available to the police and security and intelligence agencies in future as it has been in the past. I recognise that these proposals raise important issues around personal privacy. This Government is committed to ensuring that here, as elsewhere, we strike the right balance between protecting the public and safeguarding civil liberties. I believe that there are compelling reasons for the provisions in this Bill and want to ensure that they are fully considered and understood before we commence the formal legislative process.

It is for that reason that we are submitting the Bill to formal pre-legislative scrutiny by a Joint Committee of both Houses. The Intelligence and Security Committee will in parallel conduct an inquiry into the proposals. We will consider very carefully the reports by the Joint Committee, and the Intelligence and Security Committee before introducing the Bill in Parliament later in the session.

THERESA MAY

COMMUNICATIONS DATA: INTRODUCTION

Communications data is information about a communication. The term is carefully defined in existing legislation and described in codes of practice and includes data about a subscriber to a mobile phone or email account, the time, duration, originator and recipient of a communication and the location of a communication device from which a communication is made.

Communications data is very different from communications content – for example, the text of an email or a telephone conversation, and arrangements for the police and security agencies to intercept the content of a communication are very different from arrangements to get access to communications data.

Communications data is widely used by the police and other public authorities around the world. In this country it has played a vital role in counter-terrorism and serious crime cases. It enables the police to understand the activities, associates and movements of a person suspected of a crime. It can quickly identify a possible criminal network. It can also enable the police to rapidly locate people who are missing and people who are believed to be in danger.

The vast majority of communications data is accessed retrospectively, after the communications have taken place. In some cases the police need to access data in near real time, notably where lives may be at risk (e.g. during a kidnap).

Communications data is often used as evidence in Court in this country and very often plays an important role in convicting the guilty.

Companies providing communications services are currently required by law to store some communications data which they have business reasons to generate or process. They are not required to retain data which they do not need.

The police and some other public authorities can then access specified communications data held by the service providers on a case by case basis. But they must first demonstrate that the data is necessary to their investigation and proportionate to their aim and objective. The police have no power to get access to data where it is not connected to a specific investigation or operation.

Law enforcement agencies – the police, the Serious and Organised Crime Agency and Her Majesty's Revenue and Customs – account for the overwhelming majority of annual requests for access to communications data under the Regulation of Investigatory Powers Act ("RIPA") 2000. They have access to the full range of communications data. Other authorities with investigative or public protection responsibilities are able to access communications data, but most do not have access to more sensitive forms of communications data, for example data regarding the location of a mobile phone.

Local authorities account for less than 0.5% of total annual RIPA requests for communications data. Following the implementation of the Protection of Freedoms Act, they will only be able to access this data if approved by a magistrate.

Communications technologies and services are changing fast with more communications taking place on the internet using a wider range of services, including voice over internet, online gaming and instant messaging.

Communications data from these technologies is not as accessible as data from older communications systems like 'fixed line' telephones. Although some internet data is already stored by communication service providers, other data is neither generated nor obtained because providers have no business need for it.

This means that the police are finding it increasingly hard to use some types of communications data to investigate crime. To address this growing gap, the proposals set out here will require some communications service providers to obtain and store some communications data which they may have no business reason to collect at present.

Nothing in these proposals will authorise the interception of the content of a communication. Nor will it require the collection of all internet data, which would be neither feasible, necessary nor proportionate. We will extend existing safeguards regarding data retention, access and oversight. And we will remove other statutory powers with weaker safeguards under which communications data can currently be accessed by public authorities.

The following sections set out in detail the purpose and content of the legislation.

Draft Communications Data Bill

Details

Communications Data Bill

CONTENTS

INTRODUCTION

1.   This document contains a draft Communications Data Bill and Explanatory notes related to the Government's proposals to update the framework for ensuring the availability of communications data and the regulatory regime governing how public authorities obtain this data.

2.   The Explanatory Notes have been prepared by the Home Office in order to assist the reader in understanding the draft Bill and to help inform debate on it. They do not form part of the draft. References to "the Bill" in these Explanatory Notes are to the draft Bill.

3.   The notes which appear on the left-hand pages need to be read in conjunction with the Bill. They are not, and are not meant to be, a comprehensive description of the Bill. So where a clause or part of a clause does not seem to require any explanation or comment, none is given.

SUMMARY

4.   The Bill provides an updated framework for ensuring the availability of communications data and its obtaining by public authorities. It contains standard provisions in respect of, amongst other things, orders and regulations, commencement and extent. The new regime replaces Part 1 Chapter 2 of the Regulation of Investigatory Powers Act 2000 ("RIPA") and Part 11 of the Anti-Terrorism Crime and Security Act 2001 ("ACTSA") and sits alongside the Data Retention (EC Directive) Regulations 2009. The Bill is in three Parts.

5.   Part 1 makes provision for ensuring or otherwise facilitating the availability of communications data to be obtained from telecommunications operators. Clause 1 enables the Secretary of State, by order, to ensure that communications data is available to be obtained by public authorities under Part 2. Clauses 2 to 7 make express provision for safeguards in relation to Part 1. These safeguards include, by virtue of clauses 3 to 6, mandatory obligations on telecommunications operators who hold communications by virtue of this Part relating to data integrity and security, retention periods, access to the data and destruction of the data at the end of the retention period. Clause 2 imposes consultation requirements on the Secretary of State and clause 7 makes provision for further procedural safeguards, including the referral of notices to the Technical Advisory Board (established by section 13 of RIPA). Clause 8 imposes a duty, enforceable through the civil courts, to comply with requirements or restrictions imposed under Part 1.

6.   Part 2 provides for an updated scheme for the obtaining of communications data by relevant public authorities. Clause 9 enables a designated senior officer of a relevant public authority, subject to tests of necessity and proportionality, to grant an authorisation authorising the obtaining of communications data. Clauses 10 to 12 set out procedural matters in respect of such authorisations. Clause 11 provides that an authorisation made by a designated senior officer in a local authority can only take effect if approved by a relevant judicial authority. Clauses 14 to 16 and Schedule 1 enable the Secretary of State to establish, maintain and operate filtering arrangements for the purpose of facilitating the obtaining of communications data by relevant public authorities, and assisting the designated senior officer to determine whether the tests for granting an authorisation are met. These filtering arrangements may be operated directly by the Secretary of State or by a body designated by order. Clauses 17 to 21 contain supplementary provisions; amongst other things they confer a power on the Secretary of State to impose restrictions on the granting of authorisations under this Part.

7.   Part 3 contains further provisions supplementing those in Parts 1 and 2. Clauses 22 and 23 confer further scrutiny functions on the Interception of Communications Commissioner and Investigatory Powers Tribunal. Clause 24 and Schedule 2 abolish other general information powers so far as they enable public authorities to secure the disclosure of communications data from telecommunications operators or postal operators without the consent of the operator. Clause 25 applies the provisions in Parts 1 and 2 to postal operators and postal services. Clause 26 requires the Secretary of State to ensure that arrangements are in force for making appropriate contributions to postal and telecommunications operators to meet the costs incurred by them in engaging in activities permitted or required by virtue of Parts 1 and 2.

8.   Clauses 29 to 33 and Schedule 4 deal with the making of orders under the Bill, make financial provision for additional expenditure incurred as a result of the provisions in the Bill, and provide for the short title, commencement and extent.

BACKGROUND

9.   Communications data is information about a communication; it can include the details of the time, duration, originator and recipient of a communication; but not the content of the communication itself. Communications data is used by the security, intelligence and law enforcement agencies during investigations regarding national security, organised, serious and

volume crime. It enables investigators to identify members of a criminal network, place them in specific locations at given times and in certain cases to understand the criminality in which they are engaged. Communications data can be vital in a wide range of threat to life investigations, including the investigation of missing persons. Communications data can be used as evidence in court.

10.   Communications data falls into three categories: subscriber data; use data; and traffic data. The scope of these terms is set out in the Annex. Subscriber information is information held or obtained by a provider about those to whom the service is provided e.g. the name and address of the person who has subscribed to a particular phone number. Use data relates to the use made by any person of a postal or telecommunications service, for example, itemised telephone call records or itemised records of connections to internet services. Traffic data is data that is comprised in or attached to a communication for the purpose of transmitting the communications, for example, the address on an envelope or the location of a mobile phone.

11.   Given the role communications data plays in the investigation of offences and bringing offenders to justice, statutory arrangements have been in place for a number of years to ensure that it is retained by telecommunications operators and then made available on a case by case basis to designated public authorities. Part 11 of ATCSA provides a legal framework for the voluntary retention of communications data in the UK for certain purposes. The provisions in that Act are supported by a statutory code of practice ("Voluntary Retention of Communications Data under Part 11: Anti-terrorism, Crime and Security Act 2001— Voluntary Code of Practice") which came into force on 5 December 2003 by virtue of the Retention of Communications Data (Code of Practice) Order 2003 (S.I. 2003/3175).

12.   In March 2006 the European Parliament and Council adopted the EU Data Retention Directive (Directive 2006/24/EC)[1] which provided for a mandatory framework for the retention of certain communications data. This was transposed into UK law in two stages. The Data Retention (EC Directive) Regulations 2007 (S.I. 2007/2199) implemented the Directive in respect of mobile and fixed line telephony. The Data Retention (EC Directive) Regulations 2009 (S.I. 2009/859), which revoked and replaced the 2007 Regulations, implemented the Directive with respect to the retention of communications data relating to internet access, internet telephony and internet e-mail as well as mobile and fixed line telephony.

13.   The Strategic Defence and Security Review (Cm 7948)[2], published in October 2010, committed this Government to a programme to preserve the ability of the security, intelligence and law enforcement agencies to obtain communications data within the appropriate legal framework (paragraph 4.A.5).

14.   The acquisition and disclosure of communications data by law enforcement agencies and others is principally governed by Chapter 2 of Part 1 of RIPA. That Act ensures that the acquisition of communications data is in accordance with the European Convention on Human Rights ("ECHR"). RIPA enables a "relevant public authority" to make requests to obtain communications data, on a case by case basis, subject to specific tests of necessity and proportionality. The relevant public authorities are those listed in section 25(1) of RIPA or in an order made under that section (see Article 3 and Schedule 2 to the Regulation of Investigatory Powers (Communications Data) Order 2010 (S.I. 2010/480)). Any request for communications data may only be made for one or more of the purposes permitted in section 22(2) of RIPA or in an order made under that section (see Article 2 and Schedules 1 and 2 of the Regulation of Investigatory Powers (Communications Data) Order 2010 (S.I. 2010/480)). Guidance to relevant public authorities on the acquisition and disclosure of communications

---

1.   http://eur-lex.europa.eu/LexUriServ/LexUriServ.do?uri=OJ:L:2006:105:0054:0063:EN:PDF

2.   http://www.direct.gov.uk/prod_consum_dg/groups/dg_digitalassets/@dg/@en/documents/digitalasset/dg_191634.pdf?CID=PDF&PLA=furl&CRE=sdsr

data is contained in a code of practice made under section 71 of RIPA[1]. The Interception of Communications Commissioner, appointed under section 57 of RIPA, keeps under review the use of the powers in Chapter 2 of Part 1 of RIPA. Complaints about the exercise of these powers may be made to the Investigatory Powers Tribunal, established under section 65 of RIPA.

15.   A number of other enactments (for example the Social Security Fraud Act 2001 and the Financial Services and Markets Act 2000) also confer powers on certain public authorities to acquire information, including communications data. These alternative powers were considered as part of the review of counter-terrorism and security powers announced by the Home Secretary in an oral statement to Parliament on 13 July 2010 (Hansard, House of commons, columns 979 to 809; the statement was repeated in the House of Lords at columns 644 to 652). The Home Secretary reported the outcome of the review[2] in a further oral statement to Parliament (Hansard, House of Commons, columns 306 to 326; the statement was repeated in the House of Lords at columns 965 to 978). The review concluded that other statutory powers with weaker safeguards which are currently used by public authorities to acquire communications data should be removed. Lord Macdonald of River Glavan, who provided independent oversight of the review, published a separate report of his findings[3].

16.   The Bill provides for a new framework to ensure the availability of communications data and its obtaining by law enforcement agencies and other approved public authorities. This framework in respect of the retention of communications data by operators (provided for in Part 1) replaces that in Part 11 of the ATCSA, which is repealed, but sits alongside that provided for in the Data Retention (EC Directive) Regulations 2009. The new regime for the obtaining of communications data (provided for in Part 2) replaces that in Chapter 2 of Part 1 of RIPA. Amongst other things, Part 3 implements the recommendation in the review of anti-terrorism and security powers that other statutory powers with weaker safeguards which are currently used by public authorities to acquire communications data should be removed.

TERRITORIAL EXTENT

17.   The Bill extends to the whole of the United Kingdom. In relation to Scotland, Wales and Northern Ireland the provisions relate to non-devolved matters.

THE BILL

---

1.   http://www.homeoffice.gov.uk/publications/counter-terrorism/ripa-forms/interception-comms-code-practice?view=Binary

2.   http://www.homeoffice.gov.uk/publications/counter-terrorism/review-of-ct-security-powers/

3.   http://www.homeoffice.gov.uk/publications/counter-terrorism/review-of-ct-security-powers/

Communications Data Bill

CONTENTS

Supplementary provisions

PART 3

SCRUTINY AND OTHER PROVISIONS

Scrutiny of functions relating to communications data

Abolition of powers to secure disclosure of communications data

General provisions

Final provisions

EXPLANATORY NOTES

COMMENTARY ON CLAUSES

Part 1: Ensuring or facilitating availability of communications data

18.   Part 1 makes provision for ensuring that communications data is available to be obtained from telecommunications operators by relevant public authorities under Part 2, or otherwise facilitating the availability of such data to be so obtained from telecommunications operators. At present communications data may be retained by telecommunications operators because: i) it has been processed as part of their normal business, for example for marketing or billing purposes; ii) under the Data Retention (EC Directive) Regulations 2009, public communications providers are required to retain some types of telephony and internet related communications data, generated or processed in the UK in connection with their business, for 12 months; iii) certain data can be retained in accordance with a voluntary code of practice on data retention, under the ATCSA. The processing of personal information, including communications data, is regulated by the Data Protection Act 1998.

19.   The UK communications infrastructure is rapidly changing as new voice and data applications are made available over the internet. New business models and communications technologies mean that communications service providers (described as telecommunications operators in the Bill) are retaining less communications data for business purposes. Part 1 builds on existing legislation by requiring telecommunications operators to obtain and retain communications data they would not ordinarily retain for their business purposes for a period of up to 12 months. This might include data relating to i) the operator's own services which are not within the scope of existing legislation, and from which data is not otherwise retained for business purposes; ii) the services of overseas providers used by people in this country which transit systems but which the system provider currently has no business to retain. An affirmative order under clause 1 of the Bill will make provision for ensuring that communications data of this sort continues to be available to be obtained from telecommunications operators by the law enforcement agencies and other relevant public authorities.

20.   Part 1 also makes express provision for safeguards to ensure that the power in clause 1 can only be exercised following consultation with operators and furthermore that any data held by virtue of Part 1 is adequately protected and destroyed when no longer required.

Clause 1: Power to ensure or facilitate availability of data

21.   *Subsection (1)* provides for the Secretary of State by order (subject to the affirmative resolution procedure – see clause 29(2)) to ensure or otherwise facilitate the availability of communications data from telecommunications operators so that it can be obtained by relevant public authorities in accordance with Part 2. The term 'telecommunications operator' is defined in clause 28 as a person who controls or provides a telecommunication system, or provides a telecommunications service. The term 'communications data' is also defined in clause 28. In summary it is information such as telephone numbers dialled, times of calls, details of callers and receivers, and website addresses. It is not the content of the communication. The Annex provides an illustration of what communications data means for particular forms of communication.

22.   *Subsection (2)* sets out the main ways in which it is expected that the clause 1 power will be exercised. In practice, it is likely that an order under clause 1 may, amongst other things, impose requirements on operators to: generate all necessary communications data for the services or systems they provide; collect necessary communications data, where such data is available but not retained; retain the data safely and securely; process the retained data to facilitate the efficient and effective obtaining of the data by public authorities; undertake testing of their internal systems; and co-operate with the Secretary of State or other specified persons to ensure the availability of communications data.

A

BILL

TO

Make provision for ensuring or otherwise facilitating the availability of communications data and as to its obtaining by public authorities; and for connected purposes. 5

B E IT ENACTED by the Queen's most Excellent Majesty, by and with the advice and consent of the Lords Spiritual and Temporal, and Commons, in this present Parliament assembled, and by the authority of the same, as follows: —

PART 1 10

ENSURING OR FACILITATING AVAILABILITY OF DATA

Ensuring or facilitating availability

1   Power to ensure or facilitate availability of data

(1)   The Secretary of State may by order —
   (a)   ensure that communications data is available to be obtained from 15 telecommunications operators by relevant public authorities in accordance with Part 2, or
   (b)   otherwise facilitate the availability of communications data to be so obtained from telecommunications operators.

(2)   An order under this section may, in particular — 20
   (a)   provide for —
      (i)   the obtaining (whether by collection, generation or otherwise) by telecommunications operators of communications data,
      (ii)   the processing, retention or destruction by such operators of data so obtained or other data held by such operators, 25
      (iii) the entering into by such operators of arrangements with the Secretary of State or other persons under or by virtue of which the Secretary of State or other persons engage in activities on

13

23.   *Subsection (3)* provides examples of the more specific requirements that may be imposed on individual telecommunications operators or other persons under *subsection (2)*. These may include: ensuring that communications data can be disclosed without undue delay to relevant public authorities; compliance with specified standards; acquiring, using or maintaining specified equipment or systems; or using specified techniques. In practice, it is expected that requirements of this nature will be imposed by notice of the Secretary of State and will relate to particular systems and services, or classes of systems and services, provided by an operator, and particular descriptions of data.   The expectation is that notices will therefore be individually tailored to each system or service (or class of system or service) in respect of which there is an operational need for communications data to be available from an operator. The notices will describe, by reference to each service and system, the description of data which must be retained, where the data should be stored and, if necessary, how the data should be collected, generated and processed.

24.   *Subsection (4)* makes clear that nothing in Part 1 authorises any conduct consisting in the interception of communications.

Clause 2: Consultation requirements

25.   Clause 2 requires the Secretary of State to consult with a number of people prior to making an order under clause 1. These persons include OFCOM (which is the independent regulator and competition authority for the UK communications industries). The Secretary of State must also, as appropriate, consult the persons likely to have requirements or restrictions imposed on them (for example, telecommunications operators) and their representatives, the Technical Advisory Board (established by section 13 of RIPA), and bodies which have statutory functions affecting telecommunications operators. The Technical Advisory Board's makeup (as determined by the Regulation of Investigatory Powers (Technical Advisory Board) Order 2001 (S.I. 2001/3734)) includes a balanced representation of the interests of communications service providers and appropriate public authorities.

behalf of the operators on a commercial or other basis for the purpose of enabling the operators to comply with requirements imposed by virtue of this section,

    (b)   impose requirements or restrictions on telecommunications operators or other persons or provide for the imposition of such requirements or *5* restrictions by notice of the Secretary of State.

(3)   Requirements imposed by virtue of subsection (2) may, in particular, include—

    (a)   requirements (whether as to the form or manner in which the data is held or otherwise) which ensure that communications data can be disclosed without undue delay to relevant public authorities in *10* accordance with Part 2,

    (b)   requirements for telecommunications operators—

        (i)   to comply with specified standards,

        (ii)   to acquire, use or maintain specified equipment or systems, or

        (iii)   to use specified techniques,   *15*

    (c)   requirements which—

        (i)   are imposed on a telecommunications operator who controls or provides a telecommunication system, and

        (ii)   are in respect of communications data relating to the use of telecommunications services provided by another *20* telecommunications operator in relation to the telecommunication system concerned.

(4)   Nothing in this Part authorises any conduct consisting in the interception of communications in the course of their transmission by means of a telecommunication system.   *25*

(5)   In this section—

       "processing", in relation to communications data, includes its reading, organisation, analysis, copying, correction, adaptation or retrieval and its integration with other data,

       "relevant public authority" has the same meaning as in Part 2.   *30*

(6)   See—

    (a)   section 25 for the way in which this Part applies to public postal operators and public postal services, and

    (b)   section 28 for the definitions of "communications data" and "telecommunications operator" and for other definitions relevant to *35* this Part.

Safeguards

2   Consultation requirements

(1)   Before making an order under section 1, the Secretary of State must consult OFCOM.   *40*

(2)   Before making an order under section 1, the Secretary of State must consult—

    (a)   such persons appearing to be likely to be subject to the requirements or restrictions for which it provides,

    (b)   such persons representing persons falling within paragraph (a), and

Clause 3: Data security and integrity

26.   Clause 3 requires telecommunications operators to ensure that the data they hold by virtue of Part 1 is of the same quality and subject to the same security as network data, and is protected against accidental or unlawful destruction, processing, access or disclosure. These duties are consistent with those in Regulation 6 of the Data Retention (EC Directive) Regulations 2009 (S.I. 2009/859).

Clause 4: Period for which data is to be retained

27.   *Subsection (1)* of this clause requires telecommunications operators to retain the communications data they hold under Part 1 for up to a maximum of 12 months from the date of the communication concerned. The maximum period of retention is consistent with that set out in Regulation 5 of the Data Retention (EC Directive) Regulations 2009.

28.   *Subsections (2) and (3)* provides for an extension of the retention period if the telecommunication operator has been   notified by a public authority that the data is, or may be, required for the purpose of legal proceedings.

29.   *Subsection (4)* requires that the public authority must notify the telecommunications operator as soon as reasonably practicable after the authority becomes aware that the data is not required for legal proceedings.

Clause 5: Access to data

30.   *Subsection (1)* stipulates that communications data held by a telecommunications operator under Part 1 can only be accessed in accordance with the provisions in Part 2 or as otherwise authorised in law. These may include a request under section 7 of the Data Protection Act 1998 (which provides an individual with the right of access to personal data) or in pursuance of a court order.

31.   *Subsection (2)* requires the operator to put in place adequate security systems to govern access to the communications data and ensure that the data is only disclosed in accordance with subsection (1).

     (c)   such persons (other than OFCOM) with statutory functions in relation to persons falling within that paragraph,

as the Secretary of State considers appropriate.

(3)   Before making an order under section 1, the Secretary of State must consult the Technical Advisory Board.   *5*

(4)   In this section "OFCOM" means the Office of Communications.

(5)   In this Act "the Technical Advisory Board" means the Board established by section 13 of the Regulation of Investigatory Powers Act 2000.

3   Data security and integrity

A telecommunications operator who holds communications data by virtue of *10* this Part must—

    (a)   secure that the data is of the same quality and subject to the same security and protection as the data on any system from which it is derived, and

    (b)   protect the data against accidental or unlawful destruction, accidental *15* loss or alteration, or unauthorised or unlawful retention, processing, access or disclosure.

4   Period for which data is to be retained

(1)   A telecommunications operator who holds communications data by virtue of this Part must retain the data until—   *20*

    (a)   the end of—

        (i)   the period of 12 months, or

        (ii)   such shorter period as may be specified in an order under section 1 or a notice given to the operator in pursuance of such an order,   *25*

    beginning with the date of the communication concerned, and

    (b)   any extension of that period under subsection (3).

(2)   A public authority may, before the end of the period mentioned in subsection (1)(a), notify the telecommunications operator concerned that the data is, or may be, required for the purpose of legal proceedings.   *30*

(3)   If such a notification has been given, the period mentioned in subsection (1)(a) is extended until the public authority notifies the operator that the data is not required for the purpose of legal proceedings.

(4)   The public authority must, as soon as reasonably practicable after the authority becomes aware of the fact, notify the operator that the data is not required for *35* the purpose of legal proceedings.

(5)   A notification under this section must be in writing.

5   Access to data

(1)   A telecommunications operator who holds communications data by virtue of this Part must not disclose the data except—   *40*

    (a)   in accordance with the provisions of Part 2, or

    (b)   otherwise as authorised by law.

Clause 6: Destruction of data

32.   This clause provides for the destruction of communications data at the end of the period of retention, or when the data is no longer required for the purposes of legal proceedings or otherwise authorised by law. The data must be destroyed in such a way that it can never be retrieved. The deletion of data must take place within a month of the end of the retention period. The requirement to destroy data must be kept under review by the Information Commissioner as set out in clause 22(5).

Clause 7: Other safeguards

33.   Clause 7 sets out additional safeguards in relation to the power established by clause 1. It also references clauses 22, 23 and 24. Clauses 22 and 23 confer additional scrutiny functions on the Interception of Communications Commissioner, the Information Commissioner and the Investigatory Powers Tribunal. Clause 24 provides for the abolition of certain general information powers which enable public authorities to secure the disclosure by a telecommunications operator or postal operator of communications data without the consent of the operator.

34.   *Subsection (1)* sets out the procedural requirements in respect of notices provided for by an order under clause 1.

35.   *Subsections (2) and (3)* provides that an order under clause 1 must ensure that any person given a notice under clause 1(2)(b) can refer it to the Technical Advisory Board within a period specified by the Secretary of State. The Board will consider the technical requirements and financial consequences of the notice and report their conclusions to the person on whom the notice was served and to the Secretary of State. After consideration of a report from the Technical Advisory Board, the Secretary of State may withdraw the notice or issue a further notice under clause 1 confirming its effect, with or without, modifications. A further notice given following the Board's report may not be the subject of any further reference under this clause.

(2) The operator must put in place adequate security systems (including management checks and controls) governing access to the data in order to protect against any disclosure of a kind which does not fall within subsection (1)(a) or (b).

6 Destruction of data   5

(1) A telecommunications operator who holds communications data by virtue of this Part must destroy the data if the retention of the data ceases to be authorised by virtue of this Part and is not otherwise authorised by law.

(2) The requirement in subsection (1) to destroy data is a requirement to destroy the data in such a way that it can never be retrieved.   10

(3) It is sufficient for the operator to make arrangements for the destruction of the data to take place at such monthly or shorter intervals as appear to the operator to be convenient.

7 Other safeguards

(1) A notice of the Secretary of State provided for by an order under section 115 must—
  (a) be in writing,
  (b) specify the person to whom it is given, and
  (c) be given in such manner (whether by publication or otherwise) as the Secretary of State considers appropriate for bringing it to the attention 20 of the person concerned.

(2) An order under section 1 must ensure that a person, to whom a notice of the kind mentioned in section 1(2)(b) is given, can refer the notice to the Technical Advisory Board.

(3) Such an order must provide for—   25
  (a) any such reference to the Board to be made before the end of such period as may be specified in the order,
  (b) the Board to have a discretion, on such grounds as may be specified, to extend any period so specified,
  (c) there to be no requirement (other than in the case of any notice specified 30 in the order) to comply with a notice referred to the Board until proceedings on the reference are completed,
  (d) the Board—
      (i) to consider any technical matters relating to the notice referred to them and the financial consequences, for the person making 35 the reference, of the notice, and
      (ii) to report their conclusions on those matters to that person and to the Secretary of State,
  (e) the Secretary of State, after considering the Board's report, to be able to—   40
      (i) withdraw the notice, or
      (ii) give a further notice confirming its effect, with or without modifications,
  (f) a further notice given by virtue of paragraph (e)(ii) not to be the subject of a further reference to the Board.   45

Clause 8: Enforcement and protection for compliance

36.   *Subsection (1)* places a duty on a telecommunications operator, or other person, on whom a requirement or restriction is imposed by clauses 3 to 6 or a clause 1 notice, to comply with the requirement or restriction concerned. The duty to comply does not apply to a requirement or restriction imposed by a clause 1 order.

37.   *Subsection (2)* provides that if a telecommunications operator fails to comply with that duty then the Secretary of State may take civil proceedings against them for an injunction or other appropriate relief.

38.   *Subsection (3)* has the effect of making conduct lawful for all purposes if it is conduct in which a person is authorised or required to engage by virtue of this Part, and the conduct is in accordance with, or in pursuance of, the authorisation or requirement. This ensures that there is no liability attached to actions undertaken as a result of a requirement or authorisation under this Part.

39.   *Subsection (4)*(a) ensures that a person undertaking conduct that is incidental or reasonably undertaken in connection with conduct which has been authorised or required by virtue of subsection (3) is not subject to any civil liability.

40.   *Subsection (4)(b)* provides that such conduct must not be conduct for which an authorisation or warrant is capable of being granted under any of the enactments mentioned in *subsection* (5), and might reasonably have been expected to have been sought in the case in question.

Part 2: Regulatory regime for obtaining data

41.   At present, RIPA regulates how law enforcement, the security and intelligence agencies and other relevant public authorities obtain communications data from telecommunications operators. Chapter 2 of Part 1 of RIPA was enacted in order to provide public authorities with a European Convention of Human Rights ("ECHR") compliant framework for obtaining communications data. RIPA places strict rules on when, and by whom, communications data can be obtained and establishes safeguards including independent oversight by the Interception of Communications Commissioner and the Investigatory Powers Tribunal.

42.   The new scheme set out in Part 2 of the Bill preserves the essential elements of this framework. In particular, the substantive protections of Article 8 ECHR (right to respect for private and family life) will continue to be guaranteed by the express terms of Part 2 which only permit the exercise of the relevant powers if the tests of necessity, proportionality and legitimate aim are satisfied. Paragraph 5 of Schedule 4 repeals sections 21 to 25 in Chapter 2 of Part 1 of RIPA, which relate to the acquisition and disclosure of communications data.

(4) See also—

    (a) sections 22 and 23 (which confer roles on the Interception of Communications Commissioner, the Information Commissioner and the Investigatory Powers Tribunal in relation to reviewing the exercise of functions exercisable by virtue of this Part), and   5

    (b) section 24 (which abolishes certain general powers to secure the disclosure of communications data by telecommunications operators etc.).

Enforcement and protection for compliance

8 Enforcement and protection for compliance   10

(1) It is the duty of a telecommunications operator or other person on whom a requirement or restriction is imposed by—

    (a) section 3, 4(1), 5 or 6, or

    (b) a notice of the Secretary of State provided for by an order under section 1,   15

to comply with the requirement or restriction concerned.

(2) That duty is enforceable by civil proceedings by the Secretary of State for an injunction, or for specific performance of a statutory duty under section 45 of the Court of Session Act 1988, or for any other appropriate relief.

(3) Conduct is lawful for all purposes if—   20

    (a) it is conduct in which a person is authorised or required to engage by virtue of this Part, and

    (b) the conduct is in accordance with, or in pursuance of, the authorisation or requirement.

(4) A person (whether or not the person so authorised or required) is not to be 25 subject to any civil liability in respect of conduct that—

    (a) is incidental to, or is reasonably undertaken in connection with, conduct that is lawful by virtue of subsection (3), and

    (b) is not itself conduct for which an authorisation or warrant—

        (i) is capable of being granted under any of the enactments 30 mentioned in subsection (5), and

        (ii) might reasonably have been expected to have been sought in the case in question.

(5) The enactments referred to in subsection (4)(b)(i) are—

    (a) an enactment contained in Part 2,   35

    (b) an enactment contained in the Regulation of Investigatory Powers Act 2000,

    (c) an enactment contained in Part 3 of the Police Act 1997 (powers of the police and of customs officers), or

    (d) section 5 of the Intelligence Services Act 1994 (warrants for the 40 intelligence services).

Clause 9: Authorisations by police and other relevant public authorities

43.   *Subsection (1)* provides that an authorisation to obtain communications data may only be granted if a designated senior officer of a relevant public authority believes in respect of the data ("Part 2 data") that:

- it is necessary to obtain the data for a permitted purpose;

- it is necessary to obtain the data for the purposes of a specific investigation or a specific operation or for the purposes of testing, maintaining or developing equipment, systems or other capabilities relating to the availability or obtaining of communications data; and

- the conduct authorised is proportionate to what is sought to be achieved.

44.   The permitted purposes are set out in *subsection (6)* and mirror the legitimate aims in Article 8(2) of the ECHR. For example these include the interests of national security, the prevention and detection of crime or in an emergency preventing death or injury. 'Designated senior officers' are defined in clause 21 as such individuals holding ranks, offices or positions with relevant public authorities as are specified by order of the Secretary of State. Restrictions on the exercise of the power relating to granting authorisations are set out in clause 17.

45.   If the conditions in *subsection (1)* are met, *subsection (2)* provides that a designated senior officer may grant an authorisation for the designated senior officer or individuals holding offices, ranks or positions with the same relevant public authority as the designated senior officer to engage in any conduct in relation to a telecommunication system, or the data derived from a telecommunication system, for obtaining the Part 2 data from any person.

46.   *Subsection (3)* sets out a non-exhaustive list of the types of conduct which fall within clause *9(2)*. Such conduct may include the following: an authorised officer obtaining the Part 2 data themselves from any person with the consent of that person; asking any person whom the authorised officer believes is, or may be, in possession of the Part 2 data, to disclose it to an individual identified by the authorisation; asking any person whom the authorised officer believes is not in possession of the Part 2 data but is capable of obtaining the data to obtain it and disclose it to an individual identified by the authorisation; requiring by notice a telecommunications operator whom the authorised officer believes is, or may be, in possession of the Part 2 data, to disclose it to an individual identified by the authorisation; requiring by notice a telecommunications operator whom the authorised officer believes is not in possession of the Part 2 data but is capable of obtaining the data, to obtain it and disclose it to an individual identified by the authorisation.

47.   *Subsections (4)* and *(5)* set out the particular conduct that may, or may not be, authorised by an authorisation. Subsection (4) specifies that an authorisation may, for example, authorise any conduct by a person who is not an authorised officer which enables or facilitates the obtaining of Part 2 data.

48.   *Subsection (5)* makes explicit that an authorisation may not authorise the following: any conduct consisting in the interception of communications; an authorised officer to ask or require a person to disclose Part 2 data to any person other than an authorised officer or a

PART 2

REGULATORY REGIME FOR OBTAINING DATA

Authorisations for obtaining data

9   Authorisations by police and other relevant public authorities

(1)   Subsection (2) applies if a designated senior officer of a relevant public 5
authority believes in respect of communications data ("Part 2 data") —

(a)   that it is necessary to obtain the data for a permitted purpose,

(b)   that it is necessary to obtain the data —

(i)   for the purposes of a specific investigation or a specific
operation, or   10

(ii)   for the purposes of testing, maintaining or developing
equipment, systems or other capabilities relating to the
availability or obtaining of communications data, and

(c)   that the conduct authorised by the authorisation is proportionate to
what is sought to be achieved.   15

(2)   The designated senior officer may grant an authorisation for —

(a)   the designated senior officer, or

(b)   persons holding offices, ranks or positions with the same relevant
public authority as the designated senior officer,

to engage in any conduct in relation to a telecommunication system, or data 20
derived from a telecommunication system, for obtaining the Part 2 data from
any person ("section 9(2) conduct").

(3)   Section 9(2) conduct may, in particular, consist of an authorised officer —

(a)   obtaining the Part 2 data themselves from any person with the consent
of that person,   25

(b)   asking any person whom the authorised officer believes is, or may be,
in possession of the Part 2 data to disclose it to a person identified by,
or in accordance with, the authorisation,

(c)   asking any person whom the authorised officer believes is not in
possession of the Part 2 data but is capable of obtaining it, to obtain it 30
and disclose it to a person identified by, or in accordance with, the
authorisation, or

(d)   requiring by notice a telecommunications operator —

(i)   whom the authorised officer believes is, or may be, in
possession of the Part 2 data to disclose the data to a person 35
identified by, or in accordance with, the authorisation, or

(ii)   whom the authorised officer believes is not in possession of the
Part 2 data but is capable of obtaining the data, to obtain it and
disclose it to a person identified by, or in accordance with, the
authorisation.   40

(4)   An authorisation may, in particular, authorise any obtaining or disclosure of
data by a person who is not an authorised officer, or any other conduct by such
a person, which enables or facilitates the obtaining of Part 2 data.

(5)   An authorisation —

person holding an office, rank or position with the same relevant public authority as an authorised officer.

49.   *Subsection (6)* sets out the permitted purposes, consistent with Article 8(2) ECHR, for which communications data may be obtained under this Part. These may include the interests of national security, the prevention or detection of crime or for the purpose, in an emergency, of preventing death or injury. The list of purposes replicates that in section 22(2) of RIPA (which covers the purposes in subsection (6)(a), (b), (d), (e), (f), (g) and (h)) as augmented by Regulation 2 of the Regulation of Investigatory Powers (Communications Data) Order 2010 (S.I. 2010/480) (which covers the purposes in subsection (6)(i) and (j)). The purpose in subsection (6)(c) is new. The new purpose relates to the prevention and detection of any conduct in respect of which civil enforcement action for market abuse may be taken by the Financial Services Authority. It has been added to the list of permitted purposes as a result of the provisions in clause 24 and Schedule 2 which contain repeals of certain general information powers so far as they enable public authorities to secure the disclosure by a telecommunications operator or postal operator of communications data.

50.   *Subsection (7)* provides that the Secretary of State may, by order (subject to the affirmative resolution procedure – see clause 29(2)) amend subsection (6) in order to add to or restrict the permitted purposes (the power to add permitted purposes mirrors that in section 22(2)(h) of RIPA).

Clause 10: Form of authorisations and authorised notices

51.   Clause 10 makes provision for the form of authorisations and authorised notices.

52.   *Subsection (1)* sets out that the authorisation to obtain communications data must specify the conduct that is authorised and the Part 2 data in relation to which the conduct is authorised.

53.   *Subsection (2)* provides that an authorisation must specify the matters falling within the list of permitted purposes set out in clause 9(6) by reference to which the authorisation is granted, and the office, rank or position held by the person granting the authorisation.

54.   *Subsection (3)* explains that an authorisation which authorises a person to impose requirements by notice on a telecommunications operator must specify the nature of the requirements to be imposed but need not specify the other contents of the notice.

(a) may not authorise any conduct consisting in the interception of communications in the course of their transmission by means of a telecommunication system, and

(b) may not authorise an authorised officer to ask or require, in the circumstances mentioned in subsection (3)(b), (c) or (d), a person to 5 disclose the Part 2 data to any person other than—

    (i) an authorised officer, or

    (ii) a person holding an office, rank or position with the same relevant public authority as an authorised officer.

(6) For the purposes of this section it is necessary to obtain communications data 10 for a permitted purpose if it is necessary to do so—

(a) in the interests of national security,

(b) for the purpose of preventing or detecting crime or of preventing disorder,

(c) for the purpose of preventing or detecting any conduct in respect of 15 which a penalty may be imposed under section 123 or 129 of the Financial Services and Markets Act 2000 (civil penalties for market abuse),

(d) in the interests of the economic well-being of the United Kingdom,

(e) in the interests of public safety,   20

(f) for the purpose of protecting public health,

(g) for the purpose of assessing or collecting any tax, duty, levy or other imposition, contribution or charge payable to a government department,

(h) for the purpose, in an emergency, of preventing death or injury or any 25 damage to a person's physical or mental health, or of mitigating any injury or damage to a person's physical or mental health,

(i) to assist investigations into alleged miscarriages of justice, or

(j) where a person ("P") has died or is unable to identify themselves because of a physical or mental condition—   30

    (i) to assist in identifying P, or

    (ii) to obtain information about P's next of kin or other persons connected with P or about the reason for P's death or condition.

(7) The Secretary of State may by order amend subsection (6) so as to add to or restrict the permitted purposes.   35

(8) See section 25 for the way in which this Part applies to postal operators and postal services.

10 Form of authorisations and authorised notices

(1) An authorisation must specify—

(a) the conduct that is authorised, and   40

(b) the Part 2 data in relation to which the conduct is authorised.

(2) An authorisation must specify—

(a) the matters falling within section 9(6) by reference to which it is granted, and

(b) the office, rank or position held by the person granting it.   45

55.   *Subsection (4)* provides that an authorised notice must specify the following: the office, rank or position held by the person giving it; the requirements that are being imposed; and the telecommunications operator on whom the requirements are being imposed. Furthermore, the notice must be given in writing or if not in writing, then it must be in a form which produces a record of it having been given.

56.   *Subsection (5)* specifies that an authorisation for which judicial approval is required (see clause 11(1)), must be granted in writing.

57.   *Subsection (6)* provides that any other authorisation must be granted in writing or, if not in writing, in a manner that produces a record of it having been granted. An example of the latter sort of record would be a control room or operational log required to support an urgent oral grant of authorisation.

Clause 11: Judicial approval for certain authorisations

58.   This clause provides a procedure by which local authority authorisations to obtain communications data can only take effect if approved by a relevant judicial authority. The clause also provides a mechanism by which the requirement for judicial approval may be applied to authorisations granted by officials in other public authorities by order made by the Secretary of State.

59.   *Subsection (1)* provides that a local authority authorisation granted under clause 10 will not take effect until the "relevant judicial authority" has given its approval. The relevant judicial authority is defined in *subsection* (6). In England and Wales, the judicial authority is a justice of the peace, in Northern Ireland it is a district judge (magistrates' court) and in Scotland, a sheriff.

60.   *Subsection (2)* provides that notice of such applications need not be given to either the subject of the authorisation or their legal representatives.

61.   *Subsection (3)* sets out the test for the judicial approval of a local authority authorisation to obtain communications data. The relevant judicial authority must be satisfied that not only were there reasonable grounds for the designated senior officer to believe that the tests in clause 9(1) were satisfied (subsection (3)(a)(i)), but that there also remain reasonable grounds for believing so (subsection (3)(b)). The judicial authority must also be satisfied that the "relevant conditions", which relate to the authorisation or notice, were met (subsection (3)(a)(ii)). These relevant conditions are set out at *subsection* (4).

62.   *Subsection (4)* lists the relevant conditions that must be met if the relevant judicial authority is to approve the making of an authorisation. For local authorities, in England, Wales and Scotland (and in Northern Ireland where the authorisation is granted for the purpose relating to an excepted or reserved matter), these conditions are: (a) that the person granting the authorisation was a designated senior officer within the meaning of clause 21; (b) that the authorisation was not in breach of any other restrictions (see clause 17); and (c) that the authorisation satisfied any other conditions set out in an order (subject to the negative resolution procedure – see clause 29(3)) made by the Secretary of State. In relation to conditions (a) and (b), the Regulation of Investigatory Powers (Communications Data) Order 2010 (S.I. 2010/480) currently applies. For authorisations granted by public authorities other than local authorities to which the judicial approval requirement may in the future be applied, the relevant conditions are those that will be set out in an order (subject to the negative resolution procedure) made by the Secretary of State.

(3)   An authorisation which authorises a person to impose requirements by notice on a telecommunications operator must specify the nature of the requirements that are to be imposed but need not specify the other contents of the notice.

(4)   The notice itself —

    (a)   must specify —   5

        (i)   the office, rank or position held by the person giving it,

        (ii)   the requirements that are being imposed, and

        (iii)   the telecommunications operator on whom the requirements are being imposed, and

    (b)   must be given in writing or (if not in writing) in a manner that produces 10 a record of its having been given.

(5)   An authorisation to which section 11(1) applies must be granted in writing.

(6)   Any other authorisation must be granted in writing or (if not in writing) in a manner that produces a record of its having been granted.

11   Judicial approval for certain authorisations   15

(1)   An authorisation granted by a relevant person is not to take effect until such time (if any) as the relevant judicial authority has made an order approving the grant of the authorisation.

(2)   The relevant public authority with which the relevant person holds an office, rank or position —   20

    (a)   may apply to the relevant judicial authority for such an order, but

    (b)   need not give notice of the application to —

        (i)   any person to whom the authorisation which is the subject of the application relates, or

        (ii)   such a person's legal representatives.   25

(3)   The relevant judicial authority may give approval under this section to the granting of an authorisation if, and only if, the relevant judicial authority is satisfied that —

    (a)   at the time of the grant —

        (i)   there were reasonable grounds for believing that the 30 requirements of section 9(1) were satisfied in relation to the authorisation, and

        (ii)   the relevant conditions were satisfied in relation to the authorisation, and

    (b)   at the time when the relevant judicial authority is considering the 35 matter, there remain reasonable grounds for believing that the requirements of section 9(1) are satisfied in relation to the authorisation.

(4)   For the purposes of subsection (3) the relevant conditions are —

    (a)   in relation to any grant by an individual holding an office, rank or 40 position in a local authority in England, Wales or Scotland, that —

        (i)   the individual was a designated senior officer,

        (ii)   the grant was not in breach of any restrictions imposed by virtue of section 17, and

        (iii)   any other conditions that may be provided for by an order made 45 by the Secretary of State were satisfied,

63.	*Subsection (5)* allows the relevant judicial authority on refusing an approval of the grant of an authorisation to quash that authorisation. *Subsection (6)* defines various terms used in clause 11.

Clause 12: Duration and cancellation of authorisations

64.	Clause 12 limits the duration of authorisations and sets out when they must be cancelled.

65.	*Subsection (1)* provides that an authorisation ceases to have effect at the end of the period of one month beginning from the date it was granted.

66.	*Subsections (2) and (3)* permit an authorisation to be renewed at any period during the month, by following the same procedure as in obtaining a fresh authorisation. The renewed authorisation will last for a period of one month from the date the current authorisation expires.

    (b)   in relation to a grant, for any purpose relating to a Northern Ireland excepted or reserved matter, by an individual holding an office, rank or position in a district council in Northern Ireland, that—

        (i)   the individual was a designated senior officer,

        (ii)   the grant was not in breach of any restrictions imposed by virtue of section 17, and   *5*

        (iii)   any other conditions that may be provided for by an order made by the Secretary of State were satisfied, and

    (c)   in relation to any other grant by a relevant person, that any conditions that may be provided for by an order made by the Secretary of State *10* were satisfied.

(5)   Where, on an application under this section, the relevant judicial authority refuses to approve the grant of the authorisation concerned, the relevant judicial authority may make an order quashing the authorisation.

(6)   In this section—   *15*

    "Northern Ireland excepted or reserved matter" means an excepted or reserved matter (within the meaning of section 4(1) of the Northern Ireland Act 1998),

    "Northern Ireland transferred matter" means a transferred matter (within the meaning of section 4(1) of the Act of 1998),   *20*

    "relevant judicial authority" means—

        (a)   in relation to England and Wales, a justice of the peace,

        (b)   in relation to Scotland, a sheriff, and

        (c)   in relation to Northern Ireland, a district judge (magistrates' courts) in Northern Ireland,   *25*

    "relevant person" means—

        (a)   an individual holding an office, rank or position in a local authority in England, Wales or Scotland,

        (b)   also, in relation to a grant for any purpose relating to a Northern Ireland excepted or reserved matter, an individual holding an *30* office, rank or position in a district council in Northern Ireland, and

        (c)   also, in relation to any grant of a description that may be prescribed for the purposes of this subsection by an order made by the Secretary of State or every grant if so prescribed, a person *35* of a description so prescribed.

(7)   No order of the Secretary of State may be made under this section so far as it makes provision which, if it were contained in an Act of the Northern Ireland Assembly, would be within the legislative competence of the Northern Ireland Assembly and would deal with a Northern Ireland transferred matter without *40* being ancillary to other provision (whether in the Act or previously enacted) which deals with a Northern Ireland excepted or reserved matter.

12   Duration and cancellation of authorisations

(1)   An authorisation ceases to have effect at the end of the period of one month beginning with the date on which it is granted.   *45*

(2)   An authorisation may be renewed at any time before the end of that period by the grant of a further authorisation.

67.   *Subsection (4)* places a duty on the designated senior officer who has granted an authorisation to cancel it if they are satisfied that the position is no longer as set out in clause 9(1).

68.   *Subsections (5)* and *(6)* permit the Secretary of State to specify by order the person required to carry out the duty set out in subsection (4) in the event that this would otherwise fall on a person who is no longer available to perform it. This order is subject to the negative resolution procedure (see clause 29(3).

Clause 13: Duties of telecommunications operators in relation to authorisations

69.   *Subsection (1)* places a duty on a telecommunications operator who is obtaining or disclosing communications data in response to a request or a requirement for Part 2 data in pursuance of an authorisation to carry out these activities in a way that minimises the amount of data that needs to be processed for the purpose concerned.

70.   *Subsection (2)* places a duty on a telecommunications operator to comply with a requirement imposed by notice given in pursuance of an authorisation.

71.   *Subsection (3)* sets out that a person on whom the duties in subsections (1) and (2) are placed is not required to do anything in pursuance of this duty that it is not reasonably practical to do.

72.   *Subsection (4)* specifies that the duties imposed by subsections (1) or (2) are enforceable by the Secretary of State by civil proceedings for an injunction, or for the specific performance of a statutory duty under section 45 of the Court of Session Act 1988 or for any other appropriate relief.

Clause 14-16: Overview

73.   There are a number of features of internet based communications which have an impact on the acquisition of communications data by public authorities:

- The technology which is used to operate internet and mobile services, and collaboration between numerous companies may mean that communications data regarding a single communication is no longer retained in a single place. This fragmentation of data makes it difficult to obtain and aggregate all of the communications data a public authority may need to answer a specific question.

- Companies who provide internet communication services do not always require authenticated identity information, making it more difficult to identify the genuine user of a communication service. Moreover, a range of technologies are available which attempt to anonymise both the location and the identity of service users.

- Numerous mobile communication devices can be used to access Internet communication services while on the move, making it more difficult to establish from where a communication was made.

(3)   Subsection (1) has effect in relation to a renewed authorisation as if the period of one month mentioned in that subsection did not begin until the end of the period of one month applicable to the authorisation that is current at the time of the renewal.

(4)   A designated senior officer who has granted an authorisation must cancel it if   5 the designated senior officer is satisfied that the position is no longer as mentioned in section 9(1)(a), (b) and (c).

(5)   The Secretary of State may by order provide for the person by whom any duty imposed by subsection (4) is to be performed in a case in which it would otherwise fall on a person who is no longer available to perform it.   *10*

(6)   Such an order may, in particular, provide for the person on whom the duty is to fall to be a person appointed in accordance with the order.

13   Duties of telecommunications operators in relation to authorisations

(1)   It is the duty of a telecommunications operator who is obtaining or disclosing communications data in response to a request or requirement for Part 2 data in *15* pursuance of an authorisation to obtain or disclose the communications data in a way that minimises the amount of data that needs to be processed for the purpose concerned.

(2)   It is the duty of a telecommunications operator on whom a requirement is imposed by notice given in pursuance of an authorisation to comply with that *20* requirement.

(3)   A person who is under a duty by virtue of subsection (1) or (2) is not required to do anything in pursuance of that duty that it is not reasonably practicable for that person to do.

(4)   The duty imposed by subsection (1) or (2) is enforceable by the Secretary of *25* State by civil proceedings for an injunction, or for specific performance of a statutory duty under section 45 of the Court of Session Act 1988, or for any other appropriate relief.

Filtering arrangements for acquisition of data

14   Filtering arrangements for obtaining data   *30*

(1)   The Secretary of State may establish, maintain and operate arrangements for the purposes of —
   (a)   assisting a designated senior officer to determine whether, in any case, the officer believes as mentioned in section 9(1)(a), (b) and (c) in relation to the grant of an authorisation in respect of communications data, or   *35*
   (b)   facilitating the lawful, efficient and effective obtaining of Part 2 data from any person by relevant public authorities in pursuance of an authorisation.

(2)   Arrangements under subsection (1) ("filtering arrangements") may, in particular, involve the obtaining of Part 2 data in pursuance of an authorisation *40* by means of —
   (a)   a request to the Secretary of State to obtain the data on behalf of an authorised officer, and

- There are a vast range of global internet communication services. It is very easy to communicate simultaneously using multiple services and move quickly to new services.

74.   There are three broad consequences of these technical trends.

- As dependence on internet-based communications data increases, there is a risk that the utility of data may decline: it becomes harder to obtain key facts about a communications event.

- Obtaining communications data may require greater data analysis. For example, when the police need the details of the registered user of an email address, if the information cannot be obtained from the email service provider, it may be necessary to investigate more widely. Use data from the email service provider may be matched with Use and Subscriber records held by other internet companies.

- Unless otherwise regulated systems to analyse data may lead to the acquisition by public authorities of more data to identify key facts around a communication, with the potential risk of more collateral intrusion into privacy.

75.   This Bill provides for arrangements to address these issues through a filtering process, described in these explanatory notes as a Request Filter. The purpose of this Request Filter will be to:

- inform a public authority of the communications data which is available to resolve a specific enquiry; and enable that authority to judge whether in that context the request for data remains necessary and proportionate;

- obtain, process and filter communications data needed to resolve more complex requests so that only data (specified in the authorisation) which identifies the key facts about a communication is passed to a public authority; and

- protect privacy and minimise necessary interference with the rights of telecommunications users by processing the data without human intervention, and destroying any communications data irrelevant to the investigation.

76.   The powers set out in clauses 14 to 16 will provide an express statutory basis to establish and operate the new Request Filter, as well as providing additional safeguards and oversight and protecting privacy. The Request Filter can operate alongside and in addition to existing automated systems by which public authorities usually obtain communications data. The Request Filter need only be used in those cases where answering the "who, how, when and where" questions for a single communication relies on fragmented communications data and when use of the Filter is both necessary and proportionate.

77.   The powers ensure that the Request Filter will operate in accordance with the duties and privacy safeguards set out in the Bill at one remove from the police, law enforcement and security agencies. The Request Filter will be operated either by the Secretary of State or, subject to the approval of Parliament, by a designated public authority (see clause 20). Parliament will designate which public authorities will be permitted to use the Request Filter. Parliament will also set out the minimum grade of the designated senior officer within each police force or agency permitted to authorise the use of the processing and filtering functions in particular investigations.

    (b)   the Secretary of State—
        (i)   obtaining the data or data from which the data may be derived,
        (ii)   processing the data or the data from which it may be derived (and retaining data temporarily for that purpose), and
        (iii)   disclosing the Part 2 data to the person identified for this 5 purpose by, or in accordance with, the authorisation.

(3)   Filtering arrangements may, in particular, involve the generation or use by the Secretary of State of information—
    (a)   for the purpose mentioned in subsection (1)(a), or
    (b)   for the purposes of—   *10*
        (i)   the support, maintenance, oversight, operation or administration of the arrangements, or
        (ii)   the functions of the Interception of Communications Commissioner mentioned in subsection (4).

(4)   Filtering arrangements must involve the generation and retention of such *15* information or documents as the Interception of Communications Commissioner considers appropriate for the purposes of the functions of the Commissioner in relation to the arrangements under section 57(2)(e) of the Regulation of Investigatory Powers Act 2000 (review functions: see section 22 of this Act).   *20*

78.   Operation and oversight of the Request Filter requires further information to function effectively and to support and maintain the proposed statutory safeguards. This information is not communications data and is explained in paragraphs 85 and 86 below.

79.   Operation of the filtering arrangements will be overseen by the Interception of Communications Commissioner (see clause 22).

Clause 14: Filtering arrangements for acquisition of data

80.   Clause 14 provides a power to establish filtering arrangements to facilitate the lawful, efficient and effective obtaining of communications data by relevant public authorities and to assist a designated senior officer in each public authority to determine whether he believes the tests for granting an authorisation to obtain data have been met. The filtering arrangements will minimise the interference with Article 8(1) rights to which requests for internet based communications data will give rise thereby ensuring that privacy is properly protected. "Filtering Arrangements" is defined in clause 21(1) as arrangements under clause 14(1).

81.   The power to establish filtering arrangements in *subsection (1)* operates solely in the context of Part 2 of the Bill which creates a regulatory regime for obtaining data. The power is intended to facilitate the obtaining of data in particular cases by public authorities in accordance with an authorisation under clause 9 whilst protecting privacy. Any communications data obtained by the filtering arrangements must be immediately destroyed in such a way that it can never be retrieved once the purposes of the authorisation have been met. The power will be exercised in two main ways.

82.   First, the Request Filter under clause 14(1) will provide the designated senior officer with assistance in determining whether he believes the tests for granting an authorisation are met in any particular case. The Request Filter may: a) provide details of different options the Request Filter may employ to provide a response to a specific public authority data request; and b) for each identified option, provide details of the anticipated levels of interference and the likely precision of the returned results. The information provided by the Request Filter will enable the designated senior officer to understand how the Filter will answer particular questions, and will guide him through the process of determining which questions he believes it is necessary and proportionate to ask, taking into account the filtering and processing which will be undertaken and the volume of filtered data which will be disclosed.

83.   Second, if the designated senior officer grants the authorisation, the Request Filter will facilitate where necessary the efficient and effective obtaining of required Part 2 data under the authorisation on behalf of investigators whilst minimising any interference with the privacy of those whose data is processed and disclosed. As explained above, the Request Filter will be operated at arm's length from the investigation under the oversight of the Interception of Communications Commissioner by virtue of clause 22.

84.   In accordance with *subsection (2),* the Filter will:

- automate the obtaining of communications under an authorisation in response to a lawful, authorised data request from a public authority. Where extra data has to be obtained by the filter in order to obtain the data which has been requested, this extra data will only be available to the filter and will not be disclosed to the requesting public authority;

- where necessary process the obtained communications data to obtain the data which has been requested; and

- disclose to the public authority only the requested filtered Part 2 data specified in the authorisation which is required to answer the request. The duties imposed under clause 16 will ensure that the Request Filter can only ever disclose the filtered Part 2

data necessary to answer a particular request. Once the filter has provided the answer to the question to the public authority, all other data relating to the request must be destroyed in such a way that it can never be retrieved.

85.   *Subsection (3)* further provides that the exercise of the clause 14 power may, in particular, provide for the generation or use of certain categories of additional information.

86.   Aside from communications data, any new processing and filtering capability under Part 2 will require some additional information to assist the designated senior officer in determining whether the tests for granting an authorisation are met and to provide audit and oversight information to the operator of the Request Filter and the Interception of Communications Commissioner. This information is specified in *subsection (3)(a) and (b)* and may include:

- information about the type and volume of data likely to be obtained by the Filter in any particular case to ensure that the designated senior officer can assess the anticipated levels of interference, and make an informed decision as to whether he believes it is necessary and proportionate to obtain the data;

- audit and management information relating to the use made of the Request Filter to enable administrative, financial and security oversight to be exercised on a day-to-day basis; and

- information required by the Interception Commissioner to keep under review and report on the proper operation of the Request Filter.

87.   *Subsection (3)* ensures that express statutory provision is made for this additional information, and that the use of such information is subject to appropriate safeguards. Part 2 ensures, in particular, that information of this type can only be disclosed for the limited set of purposes set out on in clause 16(2).

88.   *Subsection (4)* specifies that provision must be made for the generation and retention of information or documents which are needed by the Interception of Communications Commissioner to carry out his functions. These functions are inserted into RIPA by clause 22.

Clause 15: Use of filtering arrangements in pursuance of an authorisation

89.   Clause 15 will apply in relation to the use of any Request Filter established under the power in clause 14.

90.   The effect of *subsection (2)* is that any Request Filter may be used to obtain, process and disclose Part 2 data if, but only if, these uses have been specifically authorised by the authorisation.

91.   *Subsection (3)* sets out the matters which the designated senior officer must record within the authorisation to obtain Part 2 data. These include: a) whether the Part 2 data may be obtained and disclosed by use of the filter; b) whether the processing of data under the filter is allowed; c) if the processing of data is allowed, then a description of data that may be processed must also be included.

92.   *Subsection (4)* prevents a designated senior officer from authorising the use of a Request Filter, either to obtain or process the data, unless satisfied that it is proportionate to do so.

15   Use of filtering arrangements in pursuance of an authorisation

(1)   This section applies in relation to the use of the filtering arrangements in pursuance of an authorisation.

(2)   The filtering arrangements may be used—

(a)   to obtain and disclose Part 2 data in pursuance of an authorisation, only   5
if the authorisation specifically authorises the use of the arrangements
to obtain the data,

(b)   to process data in pursuance of an authorisation (and to retain the data
temporarily for that purpose), only if the authorisation specifically
authorises processing data of that description under the arrangements 10
(and their temporary retention for that purpose).

(3)   The authorisation must record the designated senior officer's decision as to—

93.   *Subsections (2) to (4)* will accordingly ensure that the use of any Request Filter under Part 2 is specifically authorised by the authorisation, is proportionate and is recorded within the authorisation.

Clause 16: Duties in connection with operation of filtering arrangements

94.   *Clause 16* imposes duties in connection with the operation of filtering arrangements under clause 14.

95.   In the case of a Request Filter, *subsection (1)* provides that no communications data must be obtained or processed under the filter except for the purposes of an authorisation. Data which has been obtained or processed under the filter, and is to be disclosed in accordance with the authorisation or for the purposes of assisting the designated senior officer, shall only be disclosed to authorised individuals. Further, subsection (1)(c) specifically requires any data obtained by the filter to be immediately destroyed in such a way that it can never be retrieved, once the purposes of the authorisation or of the assistance function have been met or if at any time it ceases to be necessary to retain the data for these purposes.

96.   *Subsection (1)* will ensure that only the filtered data relevant to the investigation is disclosed to the requesting agency. Once the filter has provided the answer to the question, all the data relating to the request will be destroyed by the filter in such a way that it can never be retrieved.

97.   *Subsection (2)* limits the disclosure of the additional subsidiary information explained in paragraph 85 above: a) to assist a designated senior officer to determine whether he believes the tests for granting an authorisation are met; b) for the purposes of support, maintenance, oversight, operation or administration; c) to the Interception of Communications Commissioner for the purposes of any his functions; d) as otherwise authorised by law.

98.   *Subsection (3)* requires strict limits to be placed on the persons who are permitted to read, obtain or otherwise process data for the purposes of support, maintenance, oversight, operation or administration in connection with the Request Filter. No other persons must be permitted to access or use the capability except in pursuance of an authorisation or to assist the designated senior officer to determine whether an authorisation is necessary and proportionate.

99.   *Subsection (4)* requires that an adequate security system is in place to protect against any abuse of access to the Filter, as well as measures to protect against any unauthorised or unlawful data retention, processing, access or disclosure. The duty in *subsection (4)* will ensure that a Request Filter can only be used in accordance with Part 2 and is subject to adequate and effective safeguards against abuse.

100.   *Subsection (5)(a)* requires procedures to be put in place and maintained to ensure that the any Request Filter is functioning properly, including regular testing of the relevant software and hardware. *Subsection (5)(b)* requires a report to be made, as soon as possible after the end of each calendar year, to the Interception of Communications Commissioner about the functioning of the Request Filter during that year. Such a report must, in particular,

> (a) whether the Part 2 data to be obtained and disclosed in pursuance of the authorisation may be obtained and disclosed by use of the filtering arrangements,
>
> (b) whether the processing of data under the filtering arrangements (and its temporary retention for that purpose) is authorised, 5
>
> (c) if the processing of data under the filtering arrangements is authorised, the description of data that may be processed.

(4) A designated senior officer must not authorise—

> (a) use of the filtering arrangements, or
>
> (b) processing under the filtering arrangements, 10

unless satisfied that what is authorised is proportionate in relation to what is sought to be achieved.

16 Duties in connection with operation of filtering arrangements

(1) The Secretary of State must secure—

> (a) that no authorisation data is obtained or processed under the filtering 15 arrangements except for the purposes of an authorisation,
>
> (b) that data which—
>
> > (i) has been obtained or processed under the filtering arrangements, and
> >
> > (ii) is to be disclosed in pursuance of an authorisation or for the 20 purpose mentioned in section 14(1)(a),
>
> is disclosed only to the person to whom the data is to be disclosed in pursuance of the authorisation or (as the case may be) to the designated senior officer concerned,
>
> (c) that any authorisation data which is obtained under the filtering 25 arrangements in pursuance of an authorisation is immediately destroyed in such a way that it can never be retrieved—
>
> > (i) when the purposes of the authorisation have been met, or
> >
> > (ii) if at any time it ceases to be necessary to retain the data for the purposes or purpose concerned. 30

(2) The Secretary of State must secure that data (other than authorisation data) which is retained under the filtering arrangements is disclosed only—

> (a) for the purpose mentioned in section 14(1)(a),
>
> (b) for the purposes of support, maintenance, oversight, operation or administration of the arrangements, 35
>
> (c) to the Interception of Communications Commissioner for the purposes of the functions of the Commissioner mentioned in section 14(4), or
>
> (d) otherwise as authorised by law.

(3) The Secretary of State must secure—

> (a) that only the Secretary of State and individuals authorised by the 40 Secretary of State are permitted to read, obtain or otherwise process data for the purposes of support, maintenance, oversight, operation or administration of the filtering arrangements, and
>
> (b) that no other persons are permitted to access or use the filtering arrangements except in pursuance of an authorisation or for the 45 purpose mentioned in section 14(1)(a).

(4) The Secretary of State must—

contain information about destruction of data during that year (*subsection (6)*). *Subsections (5) and (6)* will ensure that the operation of any Request Filter is subject to rigorous oversight and control.

101.   *Subsection (7)* requires any significant processing errors to be immediately reported to the Interception of Communications Commissioner. *Subsection (7)* constitutes a further safeguard with respect to the operation of any Request Filter.

Clause 17: Power to impose restrictions on exercise of powers

102.   *Subsection (1)* provides that a designated senior officer of a local authority may not grant an authorisation for obtaining traffic data, or any communications data generated by a telecommunications operator under a clause 1 order. For example, a requirement may be imposed on an operator to generate information about a customer's name or address in circumstances where the operator's business model would not otherwise require it to do so. *Subsection (1)* will prevent local authorities from obtaining access to generated data.

103.   *Subsection (2)* confers a power on the Secretary of State by order (subject to the affirmative resolution procedure – see clause 29(2)) to impose restrictions on the granting of authorisations by designated senior officers. This broadly mirrors the equivalent power in section 25(3) of RIPA. The Order made under that power (see article 5 to 7 of the Regulation of Investigatory Powers (Communications Data) Order 2010) places a number of restrictions on the granting of authorisations, for example, local authorities may only obtain certain types of communications data (i.e. use data and subscriber data) .

104.   *Subsection (3)* provides that an order under this section may impose restrictions: a) on the authorisations that may be granted by a designated senior officer; b) on the circumstances in which, or purposes for which, such authorisations may be granted.

105.   *Subsection (4)* specifies that an order under this clause may in particular impose restrictions relating to the filtering arrangements in three areas: the public authorities that may use the arrangements; the permitted purposes for which the arrangements may be used; and the data that may be processed by means of the arrangements.

       (a)   put in place and maintain an adequate security system to govern access to, and use of, the filtering arrangements and to protect against any abuse of the power of access, and

       (b)   impose measures to protect against unauthorised or unlawful data retention, processing, access or disclosure.   5

(5)   The Secretary of State must—

       (a)   put in place and maintain procedures (including the regular testing of relevant software and hardware) to ensure that the filtering arrangements are functioning properly, and

       (b)   report, as soon as possible after the end of each calendar year, to the 10 Interception of Communications Commissioner about the functioning of the filtering arrangements during that year.

(6)   A report under subsection (5)(b) must, in particular, contain information about the destruction of authorisation data during the calendar year concerned.

(7)   If the Secretary of State believes that significant processing errors have 15 occurred giving rise to a contravention of any of the requirements of this Part, the Secretary of State must report that fact immediately to the Interception of Communications Commissioner.

Supplementary provisions

17   Restrictions on exercise of powers   *20*

(1)   A designated senior officer of a local authority in England, Wales or Scotland may not grant an authorisation for obtaining—

       (a)   traffic data, or

       (b)   any communications data generated by a telecommunications operator in pursuance of a requirement imposed by or under an order under 25 section 1.

(2)   The Secretary of State may by order impose restrictions on the granting of authorisations by designated senior officers.

(3)   An order under this section may, in particular, impose restrictions—

       (a)   on the authorisations that may be granted by a designated senior officer 30 with a specified public authority, or

       (b)   on the circumstances in which, or the purposes for which, such authorisations may be granted by a designated senior officer.

(4)   An order under this section may, in particular, as regards authorisations impose restrictions on—   *35*

       (a)   the public authorities that may use the filtering arrangements,

       (b)   the permitted purposes for which the filtering arrangements may be used,

       (c)   the data that may be processed by means of the filtering arrangements.

Clause 18: Lawfulness of conduct authorised by this Part

106.   *Subsection (1)* has the effect of making conduct lawful for all purposes if it is conduct in which that person is authorised to engage by virtue of an authorisation, and the conduct is in accordance with, or in pursuance of, the authorisation.

107.   *Subsection (2)* exempts a person from civil liability in respect of conduct which is incidental to, or reasonably undertaken in conjunction with, that authorised in *subsection (1)*. The conduct must not itself be conduct for which an authorisation or warrant: (i) is capable of being granted under the enactments referred to in *subsection (3),* and (ii) might reasonably have been expected to have been sought in the case in question.

Clause 19: Collaborating police forces in England and Wales

108.   Clause 19 sets out how authorisations may be granted across collaborating police forces in England and Wales. *Subsection (1)* provides that *subsections (2) and (3)* apply if a person is a designated senior officer by reference to an office, rank or position with an England and Wales police force and the chief officer of police of that force has entered into a collaboration agreement under section 22A of the Police Act 1996 with the chief officer of police of one or more other England and Wales police forces.

109.   *Subsections (2)* and (3) ensure that clause 9 treats collaborating police forces as if they were a single force. So subsection (2) makes provision for a designated senior officer to grant an authorisation for individuals with a collaborating force to engage in conduct to obtain Part 2 data if he or she believes that it is necessary and proportionate as set out in clause 9(1).

110.   *Subsection (3)* specifies how clause 9(5)(b) applies in this context. Clause 9(5)(b) limits the persons to whom an authorisation may authorise the disclosure of Part 2 data. *Subsection (3)* provides that clause 9(5)(b) has effect in its application to conduct under *subsection (2)* as if the reference to a person holding an office, rank or position with the same relevant public authority as an authorised officer included a reference to a person holding an office, rank or position with the same relevant public authority as the designated senior officer. The effect of this is that, in cases where an authorisation is granted by a designated senior officer in one police force ("Force A") to enable a person in a collaborating force ("Force B") to engage in section 9(2) conduct (for example asking a telecommunications operator to disclose data to another person), the person in Force B may ask the telecommunications operator to disclose the data to a person in Force A or Force B.

111.   *Subsection (4)* provides that a police force is a collaborating force if: a) its chief officer of police has entered into a collaboration agreement with another force under section 22A of the Police Act 1996, as mentioned in subsection (1)(b); and the persons holding offices, ranks, or positions with it are permitted by the terms of the agreement to be granted authorisations by the designated senior officer.

18 Lawfulness of conduct authorised by this Part

(1) Conduct is lawful for all purposes if—

    (a) it is conduct in which any person is authorised to engage by an authorisation, and

    (b) the conduct is in accordance with, or in pursuance of, the authorisation. 5

(2) A person (whether or not the person so authorised) shall not be subject to any civil liability in respect of conduct that—

    (a) is incidental to, or is reasonably undertaken in connection with, conduct that is lawful by virtue of subsection (1), and

    (b) is not itself conduct for which an authorisation or warrant— 10

        (i) is capable of being granted under any of the enactments mentioned in subsection (3), and

        (ii) might reasonably have been expected to have been sought in the case in question.

(3) The enactments referred to in subsection (2)(b)(i) are— 15

    (a) an enactment contained in this Part,

    (b) an enactment contained in the Regulation of Investigatory Powers Act 2000,

    (c) an enactment contained in Part 3 of the Police Act 1997 (powers of the police and of customs officers), or 20

    (d) section 5 of the Intelligence Services Act 1994 (warrants for the intelligence services).

19 Collaborating police forces in England and Wales

(1) Subsections (2) and (3) apply if—

    (a) a person is a designated senior officer by reference to an office, rank or 25 position with an England and Wales police force, and

    (b) the chief officer of police of that force has entered into a collaboration agreement under section 22A of the Police Act 1996 which contains force collaboration provision.

(2) The designated senior officer may grant an authorisation for persons holding 30 offices, ranks or positions with a collaborating force to engage in any section 9(2) conduct if the designated senior officer believes as mentioned in section 9(1)(a), (b) and (c).

(3) In its application to such conduct, section 9(5)(b) has effect as if the reference to a person holding an office, rank or position with the same relevant public 35 authority as an authorised officer included a reference to a person holding an office, rank or position with the same relevant public authority as the designated senior officer.

(4) For the purposes of this section a police force is a collaborating force if—

    (a) its chief officer of police is a party to the agreement mentioned in 40 subsection (1)(b), and

    (b) the persons holding offices, ranks or positions with it are permitted by the terms of the agreement to be granted authorisations by the designated senior officer or (as the case may be) to be identified by, or in accordance with, such authorisations. 45

(5) In this section—

112.   *Subsection (5)* defines "England and Wales police force" for the purposes of this clause.

Clause 20 and Schedule 1: Certain transfer and agency arrangements with public authorities

113.   Clause 20 and Schedule 1 cater for the possibility that the functions of the Secretary of State under clauses 14 to 16 may, at some point in the future, be transferred to another public authority designated by order, or that a public authority may carry out agency arrangements with the Secretary of State in relation to other matters falling within Part 2. In practice, the Secretary of State or designated public authority may contract with an approved body to undertake the day-to-day operation of the filtering arrangements. However, legal responsibility for ensuring the effective and lawful operation of the filtering arrangements, and complying with the duties imposed by clauses 14 to 16, will remain with the Secretary of State or other designated public authority.

114.   *Subsection (1)(a)* provides for the Secretary of State by order (subject to the affirmative resolution procedure – see clause 29(2)) to transfer responsibility to a designated public authority for the exercise of any functions under clauses 14 to 16. *Subsection (1)(b)* permits reverse transfers and transfers between public authorities. Any designated public authority would be a public authority for the purposes of the Human Rights Act 1998 (see definition of a public authority in clause 28(1)). The power in *subsection (1)* may be used to amend the constitutions of such authorities to enable them to exercise the functions concerned (see paragraph 6(1)(a) of Schedule 1). In order to enable a designated public authority to exercise these functions on behalf of the Secretary of State, *subsection (2)* provides for the Secretary of State by order to modify any enactment about a public authority. 'Modify' includes amend, repeal or revoke. This will enable the removal of statutory bars from public authorities acting as agents for the Secretary of State in relation to functions exercisable under Part 2. *Subsection (3)* provides that any order under subsection (2) does not affect the Secretary of State's responsibility for the exercise of the functions concerned.

115.   *Subsection (4)* specifies that the functions that may be exercised on behalf of the Secretary of State by virtue of *subsection (2)* do not include the function of making orders.

116.   *Subsection (5)* introduces Schedule 1 to the Bill, which contains further safeguards and provisions relating to the transfer of responsibility for the arrangements.

Clause 21: Interpretation of Part 2

117.   This clause defines relevant terms used in Part 2.

118.   A 'relevant public authority' means any of the following: a police force; the Serious and Organised Crime Agency; Her Majesty's Revenue and Customs; any of the intelligence services; and any public authority designated for the purposes of this Part by order of the Secretary of State (subject to the affirmative resolution procedure). *Subsection (7)* also provides for the Secretary of State by order to remove non-designated public authorities from the list of relevant public authorities in *subsection (1)*. For the equivalent power under RIPA, additional relevant public authorities have been designated by Article 3 of and Schedule 2 to the Regulation of Investigatory Powers (Communications Data) Order 2010 (S.I. 2010/480).

"England and Wales police force" means —

    (a)   any police force maintained under section 2 of the Police Act 1996 (police forces in England and Wales outside London),

    (b)   the metropolitan police force, or

    (c)   the City of London police force,   5

"force collaboration provision" has the meaning given by section 22A(2)(a) of that Act.

20 Certain transfer and agency arrangements with public authorities

(1) The Secretary of State may by order provide for —

    (a)   any function exercisable by the Secretary of State under sections 14 to 16 to be exercisable instead by a designated public authority, or   *10*

    (b)   any function under sections 14 to 16 exercisable by a designated public authority to be exercisable instead by another designated public authority or the Secretary of State.

(2) The Secretary of State may by order modify any enactment about a public authority for the purpose of enabling or otherwise facilitating any function exercisable by the Secretary of State under this Part to be exercisable on behalf of the Secretary of State by the authority concerned.   *15*

(3) An order under subsection (2) does not affect the Secretary of State's responsibility for the exercise of the functions concerned.   *20*

(4) Subsection (2) does not apply in relation to any function of the Secretary of State of making orders.

(5) Schedule 1 (which contains further safeguards and provisions supplementing this section) has effect.

(6) In this section and Schedule 1 —   *25*

    "designated public authority" means a public authority designated by an order of the Secretary of State,

    "modify" includes amend, repeal or revoke.

21 Interpretation of Part 2

(1) In this Part —   *30*

    "authorisation" means an authorisation under section 9 or 19,

    "authorisation data", in relation to an authorisation, means communications data that is, or is to be, obtained in pursuance of the authorisation or any data from which that data is, or may be, derived,

    "authorised officer" means a person who —   *35*

(a)   is authorised by an authorisation to engage in any section 9(2) conduct, and

(b)   either—

(i)   is the designated senior officer or holds an office, rank or position with the same relevant public authority as the   5 designated senior officer, or

(ii)   in the case of an authorisation under section 19, holds an office, rank or position with a collaborating force (within the meaning of that section),

"designated senior officers" means individuals holding such ranks, offices 10 or positions with relevant public authorities as are specified by order of the Secretary of State,

"filtering arrangements" means any arrangements under section 14(1),

"GCHQ" has the same meaning as in the Intelligence Services Act 1994,

"intelligence service" means the Security Service, the Secret Intelligence 15 Service or GCHQ,

"local authority in England" means—

(a)   a district or county council in England,

(b)   a London borough council,

(c)   the Common Council of the City of London in its capacity as a 20 local authority, or

(d)   the Council of the Isles of Scilly,

"local authority in Scotland" means a council constituted under section 2 of the Local Government etc. (Scotland) Act 1994,

"local authority in Wales" means any county council or county borough 25 council in Wales,

"member of a police force", in relation to the Royal Navy Police, the Royal Military Police or the Royal Air Force Police, does not include any member of that force who is not for the time being attached to, or serving with, that force or another of those forces,   30

"Part 2 data" has the meaning given by section 9(1),

"police force" means any of the following—

(a)   any police force maintained under section 2 of the Police Act 1996 (police forces in England and Wales outside London),

(b)   the metropolitan police force,   35

(c)   the City of London police force,

(d)   the Police Service of Scotland,

(e)   the Police Service of Northern Ireland,

(f)   the Ministry of Defence Police,

(g)   the Royal Navy Police,   40

(h)   the Royal Military Police,

(i)   the Royal Air Force Police,

(j)   the British Transport Police,

"relevant public authority" means any of the following—

(a)   a police force,   45

(b)   the Serious Organised Crime Agency,

(c)   Her Majesty's Revenue and Customs,

(d)   any of the intelligence services,

(e)   any public authority designated for the purposes of this Part by order of the Secretary of State,   50

Part 3: Scrutiny and Other Provisions

Clause 22: Scrutiny by Commissioners

119.   Under section 57 of RIPA the Interception of Communications Commissioner's current role includes oversight of the acquisition of communications data by public authorities under Chapter 2 of Part 1 of RIPA. Clause 22 amends section 57 of RIPA so as to extend the role of the Interception of Communications Commissioner to include keeping under review the exercise and performance of the powers and duties conferred by or under Part 1 and 2 of the Communications Data Bill. This does not include oversight of the following powers or duties; those under Part 1 which are subject to review by the Information Commissioner; those under Part 1 which are conferred on the Secretary of State in respect of the making of orders (see section 57(4) of RIPA) or the giving of notices; and those under Part 2 which belong to the relevant judicial authority. In practice, this means that the Interception of Communications Commissioner has responsibility for the oversight of the obtaining of communications data under Part 1 and the acquisition of this data by public authorities under Part 2. *Subsection (3)* amends section 58 of RIPA so as to place a duty on telecommunications operators, designated senior officers and other officers by or to whom an authorisation has been granted and any public authority designated under a clause 20 order to co-operate with the Interception of Communications Commissioner.

"section 9(2) conduct" has the meaning given by section 9(2).

(2)   In this Part references to crime are references to conduct that—

    (a)   constitutes one or more criminal offences, or

    (b)   is, or corresponds to, any conduct which, if it all took place in any one part of the United Kingdom, would constitute one or more criminal offences.

(3)   For the purposes of this Part detecting crime shall be taken to include—

    (a)   establishing by whom, for what purpose, by what means and generally in what circumstances any crime was committed, and

    (b)   the apprehension of the person by whom any crime was committed.

(4)   References in this Part to an individual holding an office or position with a public authority include any member, official or employee of the authority.

(5)   For the purposes of this Part information required for the purposes of supporting the filtering arrangements includes information which (to any extent) explains authorisation data.

(6)   Other expressions are defined generally for the purposes of this Part: see section 28.

(7)   The Secretary of State may by order provide for a person who is a relevant public authority otherwise than by virtue of a designation under paragraph (e) of the definition of "relevant public authority" to cease to be a relevant public authority.

(8)   The Secretary of State may by order make such amendments, repeals or revocations in this or any other enactment as the Secretary of State considers appropriate in consequence of—

    (a)   a person ceasing to be designated under paragraph (e) of the definition of "relevant public authority", or

    (b)   an order under subsection (7).

PART 3

SCRUTINY AND OTHER PROVISIONS

Scrutiny of functions relating to communications data

22   Scrutiny by Commissioners

(1)   In section 57(2) of the Regulation of Investigatory Powers Act 2000 (matters that the Interception of Communications Commissioner is to keep under review)—

    (a)   for "subsections (4) and (4A)" substitute "subsection (4)",

    (b)   the word "and" at the end of paragraph (c) is repealed, and

    (c)   after paragraph (d) insert "; and

            (e)   the exercise and performance, by the persons on whom they are conferred, of the powers and duties conferred by or under Part 1 or 2 of the Communications Data Act 2012 other than—

120.   *Subsection (5)* provides for scrutiny by the Information Commissioner of certain provisions in Part 1. The subsection places a duty on the Information Commissioner to keep under review the operation of provisions relating to data security and integrity (clauses 3(a) and (b)); the destruction of data (clause 6); and any provisions in an order under clause 1 which relate to the security of communications data held by telecommunications operators.

121.   *Subsection (6)* obliges the telecommunications operator holding data under Part 1 or 2, and the Secretary of State, to ensure that sufficient records are kept to enable the Information Commissioner, or Interception of Communications Commissioner, to discharge their duties effectively. For example, these records may include information on how telecommunications operators have responded to authorisations for obtaining communications data.

Clause 23: Scrutiny by the Investigatory Powers Tribunal

122.   *Subsection (1)* amends section 65 of RIPA so as to extend the role of the Investigatory Powers Tribunal to provide scrutiny of the new functions relating to communications data. RIPA established the Investigatory Powers Tribunal to provide for review by a judicial body of the activities of the intelligence agencies and other public authorities, including with respect to conduct by them under RIPA. The proceedings and complaints which fall within the jurisdiction of the Tribunal are set out in section 65(2) of RIPA. For example, if any person is aggrieved by conduct in relation to his communications which he believes took place under the authority of Chapter 2 of Part 1 of RIPA, he is entitled to address a complaint to the Investigatory Powers Tribunal. This Tribunal has full powers to investigate and decide any case of this nature within its jurisdiction. The Tribunal is made up of senior members of the judiciary and the legal profession and is independent of Government. The amendments to

        (i)   any powers or duties conferred by or under Part 1 of that Act which are subject to review by the Information Commissioner,

       (ii) any powers or duties conferred by or under Part 1 of that Act on the Secretary of State in respect 5 of the giving of notices, and

      (iii) any powers or duties conferred by or under Part 2 of that Act which belong to the relevant judicial authority (within the meaning of section 11 of that Act)". 10

(2)   Section 57(4A) of the Act of 2000 (exception for functions of relevant judicial authority) is repealed.

(3)   In section 58(1) of that Act (persons subject to duty to co-operate with the Commissioner) —

   (a) after paragraph (i) (and before the word "and" at the end of that 15 paragraph) insert —

      "(ia) every person on whom a power or duty has been conferred by virtue of section 4(1) or 5, or an order under section 1, of the Communications Data Act 2012,

      (ib) every person by or to whom an authorisation has been 20 granted under section 9 or 19 of that Act,

      (ic) every person to whom a notice of the kind mentioned in section 9(3)(d) of that Act has been given in pursuance of such an authorisation,

      (id) any public authority designated under section 20 of that 25 Act,", and

   (b) in paragraph (j) for "or (i)" substitute ", (i), (ia), (ic) or (id)".

(4)   In section 58(2) of that Act (duty of Commissioner to report on contraventions of Act), in paragraph (a), after "this Act" insert "or the Communications Data Act 2012". 30

(5)   The Information Commissioner must keep under review the operation of —

   (a) sections 3 and 6 of this Act, and

   (b) any provisions in an order under section 1 of this Act which relate to the security of communications data held by telecommunications operators. 35

(6)   A telecommunications operator who holds communications data by virtue of Part 1 or 2 of this Act, and the Secretary of State, must keep a sufficient record of things done by them in accordance with provision made by or under that Part to enable the Information Commissioner or (as the case may be) the Interception of Communications Commissioner effectively to discharge any 40 relevant functions.

23   Scrutiny by the Investigatory Powers Tribunal

(1)   In section 65 of the Regulation of Investigatory Powers Act 2000 (the Investigatory Powers Tribunal) —

   (a) in subsection (5) (conduct in relation to which the Tribunal has 45 jurisdiction), after paragraph (f), insert —

      "(g) conduct required or permitted by virtue of an order under section 1 of the Communications Data Act 2012

section 65 of RIPA add the following conduct to the jurisdiction of the Investigatory Powers Tribunal: conduct required or permitted by virtue of an order under clause 1 (other than conduct which is subject to review by the Information Commissioner or conduct in respect of the giving of a notice by the Secretary of State); and conduct to which Part 2 of the Bill applies.

Clause 24 and Schedule 2: Abolition of powers to secure disclosure of communications data

123.   This clause introduces Schedule 2 to the Bill which contains repeals of certain general information powers so far as they enable public authorities to secure the disclosure by a telecommunications operator of communications data without the consent of the operator. Clause 24 therefore ensures that operators are not required by law to obtain and disclose communications data other than in cases where the relevant statutory framework expressly guarantees the substantive protections of Article 8 and Directive 2002/58/EC (Directive on privacy and electronic communications).

> (other than conduct which is subject to review by the Information Commissioner or conduct in respect of the giving of a notice by the Secretary of State);
>> (h) conduct to which Part 2 of the Act of 2012 applies.",
>
> (b) in subsection (7ZA) (conduct taking place in challengeable 5 circumstances) for "23A or 32A" substitute "32A of this Act or section 11 of the Communications Data Act 2012", and
>
> (c) in subsection (8) (matters that may be challenged before the Tribunal), the word "or" at the end of paragraph (e) is repealed and, after paragraph (f), insert— 10
>> "(g) an order under section 1 of the Communications Data Act 2012;
>>
>> (h) an authorisation under section 9 or 19 of that Act; or
>>
>> (i) a notice of the kind mentioned in section 9(3)(d) of that Act." 15

(2) In section 67(7) of the Act of 2000 (powers of the Tribunal) for paragraph (aa) (but not the word "and" at the end of it) substitute—
> "(aa) an order quashing an order made under section 32A by the relevant judicial authority (within the meaning of that section);
>
> (ab) an order quashing an order made under section 11 of the 20 Communications Data Act 2012 by the relevant judicial authority (within the meaning of section 11 of that Act);".

(3) In section 68(7) of the Act of 2000 (persons subject to duty to co-operate with the Tribunal)—
> (a) after paragraph (m) (and before the word "and" at the end of that 25 paragraph) insert—
>> "(ma) every person on whom a power or duty has been conferred by virtue of section 4(1) or 5, or an order under section 1, of the Communications Data Act 2012;
>>
>> (mb) every person by or to whom an authorisation has been 30 granted under section 9 or 19 of that Act;
>>
>> (mc) every person to whom a notice of the kind mentioned in section 9(3)(d) of that Act has been given in pursuance of such an authorisation;
>>
>> (md) any public authority designated under section 20 of that 35 Act;", and
>
> (b) in paragraph (n) for "or (m)" substitute ", (m), (ma), (mc) or (md)".

Abolition of powers to secure disclosure of communications data

24 Abolition of powers to secure disclosure of communications data

(1) Schedule 2 (which contains repeals of certain general information powers so 40 far as they enable public authorities to secure the disclosure by a telecommunications operator or postal operator of communications data without the consent of the operator) has effect.

(2) Any general information power which—
> (a) would otherwise enable a public authority to secure the disclosure by a 45 telecommunications operator or postal operator of communications data without the consent of the operator, and

Clause 25: Application of Parts 1 and 2 to postal operators and postal services

124.   *Subsections (1)* and *(2)* provide for Part 1 to apply to public postal operators and public postal services as it applies to telecommunications operators and telecommunications services.

125.   *Subsections (3)* and *(4)* provide for Part 2 to apply to postal operators and postal services as it applies to telecommunications operators and telecommunication systems.

    (b)   does not involve a court order or other judicial authorisation or warrant,

is to be read as not enabling the public authority to secure such a disclosure.

(3)   The Secretary of State may by order amend, repeal or revoke any enactment in consequence of subsection (2).   5

(4)   In this section—

     "general information power" means—

       (a)   in relation to disclosure by a telecommunications operator, any power to obtain information or documents (however expressed) which—   10

           (i)   is conferred by or under an enactment other than this Act or the Regulation of Investigatory Powers Act 2000, and

           (ii)   does not deal (whether alone or with other matters) specifically with telecommunications operators or any 15 class of telecommunications operators, and

       (b)   in relation to disclosure by a postal operator, any power to obtain information or documents (however expressed) which—

           (i)   is conferred by or under an enactment other than this Act or the Regulation of Investigatory Powers Act 2000, 20 and

           (ii)   does not deal (whether alone or with other matters) specifically with postal operators or any class of postal operators,

     "power" includes part of a power.   25

(5)   References in subsections (2) and (4) to powers include duties (and references to enabling are accordingly to be read as including references to requiring).

General provisions

25   Application of Parts 1 and 2 to postal operators and postal services

(1)   Part 1 applies to public postal operators and public postal services as it applies 30 to telecommunications operators and telecommunications services.

(2)   In its application by virtue of subsection (1), Part 1 has effect as if—

       (a)   any reference to a telecommunications operator were a reference to a public postal operator, and

       (b)   any reference to a telecommunications service were a reference to a 35 public postal service.

(3)   Part 2 applies to postal operators and postal services as it applies to telecommunications operators and telecommunication systems.

(4)   In its application by virtue of subsection (3), Part 2 has effect as if—

       (a)   any reference to a telecommunications operator were a reference to a 40 postal operator, and

       (b)   any reference to a telecommunication system were a reference to a postal service.

(5)   Nothing in this Act affects any power conferred on a postal operator by or under any enactment to open, detain or delay any postal packet (within the 45

Clause 26: Operators' costs of compliance with Parts 1 and 2

126.   This clause requires the Secretary of State to make arrangements to ensure that telecommunications and postal operators receive an appropriate contribution towards such costs they incur in complying with activities permitted or required within Parts 1 and 2 as the Secretary of State considers appropriate.

127.   *Subsection (3)* provides the ability to make the payment of a contribution towards costs subject to certain conditions. *Subsection (4)* sets out such conditions may include a condition on the telecommunications or postal operator concerned to comply with an audit that may reasonably be required to monitor the claim for costs.

Clause 27 and Schedule 3: Codes of practice in relation to Part 1 and 2 functions

128.   Clause 27 introduces Schedule 3 to the Bill which makes consequential amendments to RIPA relating to codes of practice.

Clause 28: Interpretation: general

129.   This clause defines relevant terms used in the Bill.

meaning given by section 125(1) of the Postal Services Act 2000) or to deliver any such packet to a person other than the person to whom it is addressed.

26 Operators' costs of compliance with Parts 1 and 2

(1) The Secretary of State must ensure that arrangements are in force for securing that telecommunications operators and postal operators, or 5 telecommunications operators or postal operators of a particular description, receive an appropriate contribution in respect of such of their relevant costs as the Secretary of State considers appropriate.

(2) In subsection (1) "relevant costs" means costs incurred, or likely to be incurred, by telecommunications operators or postal operators in engaging in activities 10 permitted or required by virtue of Part 1 or 2.

(3) The arrangements may provide for payment of a contribution to be subject to conditions.

(4) Such conditions may, in particular, include a condition on the telecommunications operator or postal operator concerned to comply with any 15 audit that may reasonably be required to monitor the claim for costs.

(5) The arrangements may provide for the Secretary of State to determine—
    (a) the scope and extent of the arrangements,
    (b) whether or not contributions should be made to particular operators falling within the ambit of the arrangements, and 20
    (c) the appropriate level of contribution (if any) which should be made in each case.

(6) For the purpose of complying with this section the Secretary of State may make arrangements for payments to be made out of money provided by Parliament.

27 Codes of practice in relation to Part 1 and 2 functions 25

Schedule 3 (which makes provision about codes of practice) has effect.

28 Interpretation: general

(1) In this Act—
    "apparatus" includes any equipment, machinery or device and any wire or cable, 30
    "civil proceedings" means any proceedings in or before any court or tribunal that are not criminal proceedings,
    "communication"—
        (a) in relation to a telecommunications operator, telecommunications service or telecommunication system, 35 includes—
            (i) anything comprising speech, music, sounds, visual images or data of any description, and
            (ii) signals serving either for the impartation of anything between persons, between a person and a thing or 40 between things or for the actuation or control of any apparatus, and

      (b)   in relation to a postal operator or postal service (but not in the
definition of "postal service" in this section), includes anything
transmitted by a postal service,

"communications data" —

      (a)   in relation to a telecommunications operator, *5*
telecommunications service or telecommunication system,
means traffic data, use data or subscriber data, and

      (b)   in relation to a postal operator or postal service, means —

          (i)   postal data comprised in or attached to a
communication (whether by the sender or otherwise) *10*
for the purposes of a postal service by means of which it
is being or may be transmitted,

          (ii)   information about the use made by any person of a
postal service (but excluding the contents of a
communication (apart from information within sub- *15*
paragraph (i)),

          (iii)   information not within sub-paragraph (i) or (ii) that is
held or obtained by a person providing a postal service
in relation to persons to whom the service is provided
by that person, *20*

"criminal proceedings" includes proceedings before a court in respect of
a service offence within the meaning of the Armed Forces Act 2006,

"document" includes a map, plan, design, drawing, picture or other
image,

"enactment" means an enactment whenever passed or made; and *25*
includes —

      (a)   an enactment contained in subordinate legislation within the
meaning of the Interpretation Act 1978,

      (b)   an enactment contained in, or in an instrument made under, an
Act of the Scottish Parliament, *30*

      (c)   an enactment contained in, or in an instrument made under,
Northern Ireland legislation, and

      (d)   an enactment contained in, or in an instrument made under, a
Measure or Act of the National Assembly for Wales,

"interception" has the same meaning as in the Regulation of Investigatory *35*
Powers Act 2000 (see sections 2 and 81 of that Act),

"legal proceedings" means —

      (a)   civil or criminal proceedings in or before a court or tribunal, or

      (b)   proceedings before an officer in respect of a service offence
within the meaning of the Armed Forces Act 2006, *40*

"person" includes an organisation and any association or combination of
persons,

"postal data" means data which —

      (a)   identifies, or purports to identify, a person, apparatus or
location to or from which a communication is or may be *45*
transmitted,

      (b)   identifies or selects, or purports to identify or select, apparatus
through which, or by means of which, a communication is or
may be transmitted,

      (c)   identifies, or purports to identify, the time at which an event *50*
relating to a communication occurs, or

(d)   identifies the data or other data as data comprised in or attached to a particular communication,

and for the purposes of this definition "data", in relation to a postal item, includes anything written on the outside of the item,

"postal item" means —   5

(a)   any letter, postcard or other such thing in writing as may be used by the sender for imparting information to the recipient, or

(b)   any packet or parcel,

"postal operator" means a person providing a postal service,

"postal service" means a service that—   10

(a)   consists in the following, or in any one or more of them, namely, the collection, sorting, conveyance, distribution and delivery (whether in the United Kingdom or elsewhere) of postal items, and

(b)   has as its main purpose, or one of its main purposes, to make 15 available, or to facilitate, a means of transmission from place to place of postal items containing communications,

"primary legislation" means —

(a)   an Act of Parliament,

(b)   an Act of the Scottish Parliament,   20

(c)   a Measure or Act of the National Assembly for Wales, or

(d)   Northern Ireland legislation,

"public authority" means a public authority within the meaning of section 6 of the Human Rights Act 1998, other than a court or tribunal,

"public postal operator" means a person providing a public postal service, 25

"public postal service" means a postal service that is offered or provided to the public or a substantial section of the public,

"specified", in relation to an order, notice or authorisation, means specified or described in the order, notice or (as the case may be) authorisation (and "specify" is to be read accordingly),   30

"statutory", in relation to a function, means a function conferred or imposed by or under an enactment,

"subordinate legislation" means —

(a)   subordinate legislation within the meaning of the Interpretation Act 1978, or   35

(b)   an instrument made under an Act of the Scottish Parliament, Northern Ireland legislation or a Measure or Act of the National Assembly for Wales,

"subscriber data" has the meaning given by subsection (5),

"the Technical Advisory Board" has the meaning given by section 2(5),   40

"telecommunications operator" means a person who—

(a)   controls or provides a telecommunication system, or

(b)   provides a telecommunications service,

"telecommunication system" means a system (including the apparatus comprised in it) that exists (whether wholly or partly in the United 45 Kingdom or elsewhere) for the purpose of facilitating the transmission of communications by any means involving the use of electrical or electro-magnetic energy,

"telecommunications service" means a service that consists in the provision of access to, and of facilities for making use of, a 50

telecommunication system (whether or not one provided by the person providing the service),

"traffic data" has the meaning given by subsections (2) and (3),

"use data" has the meaning given by subsection (4).

(2) "Traffic data" means data— 5

(a) which is comprised in, attached to or logically associated with a communication (whether by the sender or otherwise) for the purposes of a telecommunication system by means of which the communication is being or may be transmitted, and

(b) which— 10

(i) identifies, or purports to identify, any person, apparatus or location to or from which the communication is or may be transmitted,

(ii) identifies or selects, or purports to identify or select, apparatus through which, or by means of which, the communication is or 15 may be transmitted,

(iii) comprises signals for the actuation of apparatus used for the purposes of a telecommunication system for effecting (in whole or in part) the transmission of the communication,

(iv) identifies, or purports to identify, the time at which an event 20 relating to the communication occurs, or

(v) identifies data as comprised in, attached to or logically associated with the communication.

The references in this subsection to a telecommunication system by means of which a communication is being or may be transmitted include, in relation to 25 data comprising signals for the actuation of apparatus, any telecommunication system in which that apparatus is comprised.

(3) Data identifying a computer file or computer program access to which is obtained, or which is run, by means of the communication is not "traffic data" except to the extent that the file or program is identified by reference to the 30 apparatus in which it is stored.

(4) "Use data" means information—

(a) which is about the use made by a person—

(i) of a telecommunications service, or

(ii) in connection with the provision to or use by any person of a 35 telecommunications service, of any part of a telecommunication system, but

(b) which does not (apart from any information falling within paragraph (a) which is traffic data) include any of the contents of a communication. 40

(5) "Subscriber data" means information (other than traffic data or use data) held or obtained by a person providing a telecommunications service about those to whom the service is provided by that person.

(6) Nothing in any of the provisions of this Act by virtue of which conduct of any description is or may be authorised by an authorisation or notice or an order 45 under section 1, or by virtue of which information may be obtained in any manner, is to be read—

Clause 29: Orders

130.   This clause sets out the parliamentary procedure in respect of various order-making powers provided for in the Bill.

Clause 30: Financial provisions

131.   This clause authorises out of money provided by Parliament any expenditure incurred by the Secretary of State under the Bill. It also authorises any additional expenditure incurred under any other Acts, where that additional expenditure results from the Bill.

    (a)   as making it unlawful to engage in any conduct of that description which is not otherwise unlawful under this Act and would not be unlawful apart from this Act,

    (b)   as otherwise requiring —

        (i)   the grant, giving or making of such an authorisation, notice or order, or   *5*

        (ii)   the taking of any step for or towards obtaining the authority of such an authorisation, notice or order,

    before any such conduct of that description is engaged in, or

    (c)   as prejudicing any power to obtain information by any means not *10* involving conduct that may be authorised under this Act.

Final provisions

29   Orders

    (1)   Any power of the Secretary of State or the Treasury to make an order under this Act —   *15*

        (a)   is exercisable by statutory instrument,

        (b)   may be exercised so as to make different provision for different cases or descriptions of case, different circumstances, different purposes or different areas, and

        (c)   includes power to make supplementary, incidental, consequential, *20* transitional, transitory or saving provision.

    (2)   A statutory instrument containing —

        (a)   an order under section 1, 9(7), 11(6), 17 or 20,

        (b)   an order under section 21 that —

            (i)   designates a public authority under paragraph (e) of the *25* definition of "relevant public authority" in subsection (1) of that section, or

            (ii)   amends or repeals any provision of primary legislation, or

        (c)   an order under section 24(3) or 31 which amends or repeals any provision of primary legislation,   *30*

    may not be made unless a draft of the instrument has been laid before, and approved by a resolution of, each House of Parliament.

    (3)   A statutory instrument containing —

        (a)   an order under section 11(4) or 12 or paragraph 3(1)(b) of Schedule 1, or

        (b)   an order under section 21, 24(3) or 31 to which subsection (2) above *35* does not apply,

    is (if a draft of the instrument has not been laid before, and approved by a resolution of, each House of Parliament) subject to annulment in pursuance of a resolution of either House of Parliament.

    (4)   A statutory instrument containing an order under paragraph 5 of Schedule 1 is *40* subject to annulment in pursuance of a resolution of the House of Commons.

30   Financial provisions

    There is to be paid out of money provided by Parliament —

Clause 31: Consequential provision

132.   *Subsection (1)* introduces Schedule 4 which makes consequential amendments to other enactments.

133.   *Subsection (2)* confers a power, by order, to make other consequential amendments to enactments.   To the extent that an order under this clause amends or repeals primary legislation, it will be subject to the affirmative resolution procedure, otherwise it will be subject to the negative resolution procedure (see clause 29).

Clause 32: Transitional, transitory or saving provision

134.   This clause enables the Secretary of State, by order, to make transitional, transitory or saving provisions in connection with the coming into force of the provisions of the Bill. Such an order is not subject to any parliamentary procedure.

Clause 33: Short title, commencement and extent

135.   *Subsection (1)* sets out the short title for the Bill.

136.   *Subsections (2) and (3)* provide for commencement (see paragraph 132 for further details).

137.   *Subsections (4) and (5)* set out the extent of the provisions in the Bill (see paragraph 17).

    (a)   any expenditure incurred by the Secretary of State by virtue of this Act, and

    (b)   any increase attributable to this Act in the sums payable by virtue of any other Act out of money so provided.

31   Consequential provision   *5*

    (1)   Schedule 4 (consequential provision) has effect.

    (2)   The Secretary of State may by order make such provision as the Secretary of State considers appropriate in consequence of this Act.

    (3)   The power to make an order under this section may, in particular, be exercised by amending, repealing, revoking or otherwise modifying any provision made *10* by or under an enactment.

32   Transitional, transitory or saving provision

    (1)   The Secretary of State may by order make such transitional, transitory or saving provision as the Secretary of State considers appropriate in connection with the coming into force of any provision of this Act.   *15*

    (2)   An order under subsection (1) may, in particular, make such transitory provision as the Secretary of State considers appropriate in consequence of any provision of the Police and Fire Reform (Scotland) Act 2012 not coming into force before any provision of this Act.

    (3)   Such an order may, in particular, modify—   *20*

        (a)   paragraph (a) of the definition of "relevant person" in section 11(6) of this Act to exclude an individual holding an office, rank or position in a fire and rescue authority in Scotland,

        (b)   section 19 of this Act for the purpose of making provision in relation to police forces maintained under or by virtue of section 1 of the Police *25* (Scotland) Act 1967 which corresponds to provision made by section 19 in relation to England and Wales police forces, or

        (c)   the reference to the Police Service of Scotland in the definition of "police force" in section 21(1) of this Act.

    (4)   Subsections (2) and (3) do not limit the scope of the power conferred by *30* subsection (1).

33   Short title, commencement and extent

    (1)   This Act may be cited as the Communications Data Act 2012.

    (2)   Subject to subsection (3), this Act comes into force on such day as the Secretary of State may by order appoint; and different days may be appointed for *35* different purposes.

    (3)   Sections 29, 30, 31(2) and (3) and 32 and this section come into force on the day on which this Act is passed.

    (4)   Subject to subsection (5), this Act extends to England and Wales, Scotland and Northern Ireland.   *40*

(5) An amendment, repeal or revocation of an enactment has the same extent as the enactment amended, repealed or revoked.

Schedule 1: Transfer and agency arrangements with public authorities: further provisions

138.   *Paragraph 1* provides that an order under clause 20 cannot transfer functions to a public authority without the consent of that authority. The Secretary of State must also be satisfied that the authority in question can discharge the functions effectively and in accordance with the requirements that are set out in an order, for example as to data security.

139.   *Paragraph 2* provides particular safeguards in connection with clause 16 (duties in connection with the operation of filtering arrangements). Sub-paragraph (2) requires the Secretary of State to approve the measures to be adopted by a designated public authority for complying with the requirements in clause 16. A designated public authority must send the reports required to be produced under clause 16(5)(b), or (7) to the Secretary of State as well as to the Interception of Communications Commissioner.

140.   *Paragraph 3* requires a designated public authority to make an annual report to the Secretary of State in respect of its functions under clauses 14 to 16.

141.   *Paragraph 4* sets out that the Secretary of State, in connection with an order made under clause 20, may make a scheme for the transfer of property, rights or liabilities (including rights and liabilities relating to contracts of employment). Such transfers may be from the Secretary of State (in practice, the Home Office) to a designated public authority or from one designated public authority to the Secretary of State or to another designated public authority. Paragraph 4(3) lists consequential, supplementary, incidental and transitional provision that may be made by a transfer scheme. These include making provision the same as or similar to the TUPE regulations (the Transfer of Undertakings (Protections of Employment) Regulations 2006 (S.I. 2006/246)). By virtue of subparagraph (5), a scheme may make provision for the payment of compensation, for example to a designated public authority in circumstances where functions under clauses 14 to 16 conferred on that body are brought back within the Home Office. Sub-paragraph (6) provides that a transfer scheme may either be included in an order made under clause 20 or be a standalone document; in the latter case the scheme must be laid before Parliament after being made.

142.   *Paragraph 5* provides a power for the Treasury to make an order (subject to the negative resolution procedure in the House of Commons) providing for the tax consequences of a transfer scheme made under paragraph 4. For the purposes of this power the relevant taxes are income tax, corporation tax, capital gains tax, stamp duty and stamp duty reserve tax.

SCHEDULES

SCHEDULE 1   Section 20(5)

TRANSFER AND AGENCY ARRANGEMENTS WITH PUBLIC AUTHORITIES: FURTHER
PROVISIONS

No transfer of functions without consent of transferee and suitable arrangements   5

1   No order may be made under section 20(1) transferring functions to a
           designated public authority unless the Secretary of State considers that the
           authority —
           (a)   is willing to exercise the functions concerned, and
           (b)   will have arrangements in place which are likely to ensure that the 10
                 functions will be exercised effectively and in accordance with any
                 requirements or other provision made by the order.

Particular safeguards in connection with operation of section 16

2   (1)   The following provisions apply where the functions of the Secretary of State
           under section 16 are exercisable by a designated public authority by virtue 15
           of an order under section 20(1).

     (2)   The measures adopted or arrangements made by the public authority for the
           purpose of complying with the requirements of section 16 must be such as
           are approved by the Secretary of State.

     (3)   Any report required by section 16(5)(b) or (7) must be made to the Secretary 20
           of State as well as to the Interception of Communications Commissioner.

Requirement for transferee to provide reports to Secretary of State

3   (1)   A designated public authority exercising functions by virtue of an order
           under section 20(1) must, at least once in each calendar year, make a report
           to the Secretary of State on —   25
           (a)   the discharge of the functions, and
           (b)   such other matters as the Secretary of State may by order require.

     (2)   An order under section 20(1) may, in particular, modify sub-paragraph (1)
           as it has effect in relation to the calendar year in which the order comes into
           force or is revoked.   30

     (3)   The Secretary of State may agree to a report under this paragraph being
           combined with any other report which the authority is required to, or may,
           make to the Secretary of State.

Transfer schemes in connection with transfer of functions

4   (1)   The Secretary of State may, in connection with an order under section 20(1), 35
           make a scheme for the transfer of property, rights or liabilities.

     (2)   The things that may be transferred under a transfer scheme include —
           (a)   property, rights and liabilities which could not otherwise be
                 transferred,

    (b)   property acquired, and rights and liabilities arising, after the making of the scheme.

(3) A transfer scheme may make consequential, supplementary, incidental, transitional, transitory or saving provision and may, in particular —

    (a)   create rights, or impose liabilities, in relation to property or rights *5* transferred,

    (b)   make provision about the continuing effect of things done by, on behalf of or in relation to the transferor in respect of anything transferred,

    (c)   make provision about the continuation of things (including legal *10* proceedings) in the process of being done by, on behalf of or in relation to the transferor in respect of anything transferred,

    (d)   make provision for references to the transferor in an instrument or other document in respect of anything transferred to be treated as references to the transferee, *15*

    (e)   make provision for the shared ownership or use of property,

    (f)   if the TUPE regulations do not apply in relation to the transfer, make provision which is the same or similar.

(4) A transfer scheme may provide —

    (a)   for modification by agreement, *20*

    (b)   for modifications to have effect from the date when the original scheme came into effect.

(5) A transfer scheme may confer a discretion on the Secretary of State to pay compensation to any person whose interests are adversely affected by the scheme. *25*

(6) A transfer scheme may be included in an order under section 20(1) but, if not so included, must be laid before Parliament after being made.

(7) For the purposes of this section references to rights and liabilities include references to —

    (a)   rights and liabilities relating to a contract of employment, and *30*

    (b)   rights and liabilities of the Crown relating to the terms of employment of individuals in the civil service.

(8) Accordingly, a transfer scheme may, in particular, provide —

    (a)   for —

        (i)   an individual employed in the civil service to become an *35* employee of the transferee, or

        (ii)   an employee of the transferor to become an employee of the transferee or an individual employed in the civil service,

    (b)   for —

        (i)   the individual's terms of employment in the civil service to *40* have effect (subject to any necessary modifications) as the terms of the individual's contract of employment with the transferee, or

        (ii)   (as the case may be) the individual's contract of employment to have effect (subject to any necessary modifications) as the *45* terms of the individual's contract of employment with the transferee or, where the transferee is the Secretary of State, the individual's terms of employment with the civil service,

(c)   for the transfer of rights and liabilities of the Crown or another public authority under or in connection with the individual's terms of employment.

(9) In this paragraph—

"civil service" means the civil service of the State,   5

"TUPE regulations" means the Transfer of Undertakings (Protection of Employment) Regulations 2006 (S.I. 2006/246),

references to the transfer of property include the grant of a lease.

Tax in connection with transfer schemes

5   (1) The Treasury may by order make provision varying the way in which a 10 relevant tax has effect in relation to—

(a)   anything transferred under a transfer scheme, or

(b)   anything done for the purposes of, or in relation to, a transfer under a transfer scheme.

(2) The provision which may be made under sub-paragraph (1)(a) includes, in 15 particular, provision for—

(a)   a tax provision not to apply, or to apply with modifications, in relation to anything transferred,

(b)   anything transferred to be treated in a specified way for the purposes of a tax provision,   20

(c)   the Secretary of State to be required or permitted to determine, or specify the method for determining, anything which needs to be determined for the purposes of any tax provision so far as relating to anything transferred.

(3) The provision which may be made under sub-paragraph (1)(b) includes, in 25 particular, provision for—

(a)   a tax provision not to apply, or to apply with modifications, in relation to anything done for the purposes of, or in relation to, the transfer,

(b)   anything done for the purposes of, or in relation to, the transfer to 30 have or not have a specified consequence or be treated in a specified way,

(c)   the Secretary of State to be required or permitted to determine, or specify the method for determining, anything which needs to be determined for the purposes of any tax provision so far as relating to 35 anything done for the purposes of, or in relation to, the transfer.

(4) In this paragraph—

"relevant tax" means income tax, corporation tax, capital gains tax, stamp duty, stamp duty reserve tax or stamp duty land tax,

"tax provision" means any provision—   40

(a)   about a relevant tax, and

(b)   made by an enactment,

"transfer scheme" means a transfer scheme under paragraph 4,

and references to the transfer of property include the grant of a lease.

Schedule 2: Abolition of Disclosure Powers

143.   Schedule 2 contains repeals of certain general information powers so far as they enable public authorities to secure the disclosure by a telecommunications operator of communications data without the consent of the operator.

Supplementary and other general provision

6   (1) The power to make an order under section 20(1) includes, in particular, power to —

(a)   modify any enactment about a public authority for the purpose of enabling or otherwise facilitating any function under sections 14 to 5 16 to be exercisable by the authority,

(b)   impose requirements or confer other functions on a public authority in connection with functions transferred by the order.

7   The power to make an order under —

(a)   section 20, or   10

(b)   paragraph 5 above,

including that power as extended (whether by section 29(1) or otherwise) may, in particular, be exercised by modifying any enactment (including this Act).

SCHEDULE 2   Section 24(1) 15

ABOLITION OF DISCLOSURE POWERS

Trade Descriptions Act 1968 (c. 29)

1   In section 28 of the Trade Descriptions Act 1968 (power to enter premises and inspect and seize goods and documents), at end, insert —

"(8)   Nothing in this section is to be read as enabling an officer to secure 20 the disclosure by a telecommunications operator or postal operator of communications data without the consent of the operator.

(9)   In subsection (8) "communications data", "postal operator" and "telecommunications operator" have the same meanings as in the Communications Data Act 2012 (see section 28 of that Act)."   25

Health and Safety at Work etc. Act 1974 (c. 37)

2   In section 20 of the Health and Safety at Work etc. Act 1974 (powers of inspectors), at end, insert —

"(9)   Nothing in this section is to be read as enabling an inspector to secure the disclosure by a telecommunications operator or postal operator 30 of communications data without the consent of the operator.

(10)   In subsection (9) "communications data", "postal operator" and "telecommunications operator" have the same meanings as in the Communications Data Act 2012 (see section 28 of that Act)."

Criminal Justice Act 1987 (c. 38)   35

3   In section 2 of the Criminal Justice Act 1987 (investigation powers of

Director of Serious Fraud Office), after subsection (10), insert—

"(10A) Nothing in this section is to be read as enabling a person to secure the disclosure by a telecommunications operator or postal operator of communications data without the consent of the operator.

(10B) In subsection (10A) "communications data", "postal operator" and "telecommunications operator" have the same meanings as in the Communications Data Act 2012 (see section 28 of that Act)." 5

Consumer Protection Act 1987 (c. 43)

4   In section 29 of the Consumer Protection Act 1987 (powers of search etc.), at end, insert— 10

"(8)   The officer may not exercise a power under this section to secure the disclosure by a telecommunications operator or postal operator of communications data without the consent of the operator.

(9)   In subsection (8) "communications data", "postal operator" and "telecommunications operator" have the same meanings as in the 15 Communications Data Act 2012 (see section 28 of that Act)."

Environmental Protection Act 1990 (c. 43)

5   In section 71 of the Environmental Protection Act 1990 (obtaining of information from persons and authorities), at end, insert—

"(5)   Nothing in this section is to be read as enabling a person to secure the 20 disclosure by a telecommunications operator or postal operator of communications data without the consent of the operator.

(6)   In subsection (5) "communications data", "postal operator" and "telecommunications operator" have the same meanings as in the Communications Data Act 2012 (see section 28 of that Act)." 25

Social Security Administration Act 1992 (c. 5)

6   In section 109B of the Social Security Administration Act 1992 (power to require information)—
        (a) in subsection (2A), paragraph (j) is repealed,
        (b) in subsection (2E), for the words from "for" to the end of the 30 subsection substitute "so as to secure the disclosure by a telecommunications operator or postal operator of communications data without the consent of the operator.",
        (c) subsection (2F) is repealed, and
        (d) in subsection (7)— 35
              (i)   after the definition of "bank" insert—
                    ""communications data" has the same meaning as in the Communications Data Act 2012 (see section 28 of that Act);",
              (ii) after the definition of "insurer" insert— 40
                    ""postal operator" has the same meaning as in the Communications Data Act 2012 (see section 28 of that Act);", and

   (iii) for the definition of "telecommunications service"
     substitute—

      ""telecommunications operator" has the same meaning
      as in the Communications Data Act 2012 (see section
      28 of that Act);".   *5*

7   In section 109C of the Social Security Administration Act 1992 (powers of
   entry), for subsection (6), substitute—

   "(6) Subsections (2E) and (5) of section 109B apply for the purposes of this
     section as they apply for the purposes of that section."

Competition Act 1998 (c. 41)   *10*

8   In section 26 of the Competition Act 1998 (powers of the Office of Fair
   Trading when conducting investigations), after subsection (6), insert—

   "(7) Nothing in this section is to be read as enabling the OFT to secure the
     disclosure by a telecommunications operator or postal operator of
     communications data without the consent of the operator. *15*

   (8) In subsection (7) "communications data", "postal operator" and
     "telecommunications operator" have the same meanings as in the
     Communications Data Act 2012 (see section 28 of that Act)."

Financial Services and Markets Act 2000 (c. 8)

9   In section 175 of the Financial Services and Markets Act 2000 (information *20*
   gathering and investigations: supplemental provision), after subsection (5),
   insert—

   "(5A) Nothing in this Part is to be read as enabling a person to secure the
     disclosure by a telecommunications operator or postal operator of
     communications data without the consent of the operator. *25*

   (5B) In subsection (5A) "communications data", "postal operator" and
     "telecommunications operator" have the same meanings as in the
     Communications Data Act 2012 (see section 28 of that Act)."

Enterprise Act 2002 (c. 40)

10   In section 224 of the Enterprise Act 2002 (enforcement of consumer *30*
   legislation: information gathering powers of the Office of Fair Trading), at
   end, insert—

   "(3) Nothing in this section is to be read as enabling the OFT to secure the
     disclosure by a telecommunications operator or postal operator of
     communications data without the consent of the operator. *35*

   (4) In subsection (3) "communications data", "postal operator" and
     "telecommunications operator" have the same meanings as in the
     Communications Data Act 2012 (see section 28 of that Act)."

11   In section 225 of the Enterprise Act 2002 (enforcement of consumer
   legislation: information gathering powers of certain enforcers), at end, *40*

Schedule 3: Codes of Practice in relation to Part 1 and 2 Functions

144.   *Paragraph 2* of Schedule 3 makes consequential amendments to section 71(2) of RIPA to require codes of practice to be issued under that section in respect of the powers and duties under Parts 1 and 2 of the Bill. Codes issued under section 71 are subject to the affirmative resolution procedure.

145.   *Paragraph 3* of Schedule 3 amends the procedure in section 71 of RIPA for issuing codes of practice under the Act. These changes respond to concerns raised by the Joint Committee on Statutory Instruments in its 30th Report of Session 2002/2003 concerning S.I. 2003/3175 made under equivalent powers in section 103 of the Anti-terrorism Crime and Security Act 2001.

146.   *Paragraph 6* of Schedule 3 inserts new section 71A into RIPA. The new section is designed to simplify the procedure for revising codes of practice issued under section 71. Practical experience following the enactment of RIPA suggests that the codes of practice need to be revised on a far more regular basis than had originally been envisaged. By way of example, codes of practice which mention relevant public authorities or specify authorisation levels for particular activities quickly become out of date when bodies are abolished or merge following machinery of government and other changes. In many cases, however, the substance of the code remains the same and does not require any significant revisions.

147.   New section 71A of RIPA accordingly provides that an order bringing a revision of a code of practice into operation may either be subject to the affirmative resolution procedure or must be laid before Parliament. In both cases, the Secretary of State must first publish the code in draft and consider any representation made about it, and must lay the modified code before Parliament together with the order to which it relates.

insert—

    "(4)   Nothing in this section is to be read as enabling an enforcer to secure the disclosure by a telecommunications operator or postal operator of communications data without the consent of the operator.

    (5)   In subsection (4) "communications data", "postal operator" and "telecommunications operator" have the same meanings as in the Communications Data Act 2012 (see section 28 of that Act)."

Finance Act 2008 (c. 9)

12   In Schedule 36 to the Finance Act 2008 (information and inspection powers), in paragraph 19 (restrictions on powers: types of information), at end, insert—

    "(4)   An information notice does not require a telecommunications operator or postal operator to provide or produce communications data.

    (5)   In sub-paragraph (4) "communications data", "postal operator" and "telecommunications operator" have the same meanings as in the Communications Data Act 2012 (see section 28 of that Act)."

SCHEDULE 3

Section 27

CODES OF PRACTICE IN RELATION TO PART 1 AND 2 FUNCTIONS

1   The Regulation of Investigatory Powers Act 2000 is amended as follows.

2   In section 71(2) (issue and revision of codes of practice: powers and duties in respect of which code of practice must be issued)—

    (a)   for "subsection (10)" substitute "subsections (10) and (11)",

    (b)   for "of section 23A or 32A" substitute "given by section 32A(7) of this Act or section 11(6) of the Communications Data Act 2012",

    (c)   the word "and" at the end of paragraph (b) is repealed, and

    (d)   after paragraph (c) insert "; and

        "(d)   Parts 1 and 2 of the Communications Data Act 2012."

3   For subsections (3) to (9) of section 71 substitute—

    "(3)   Before issuing a code the Secretary of State must—

        (a)   prepare and publish a draft of the code, and

        (b)   consider any representations made about it,

    and may modify the draft.

    (4)   A code does not come into operation until the Secretary of State by order so provides.

    (5)   An order bringing a code into operation may not be made unless a draft of the order has been laid before Parliament and approved by a resolution of each House.

    (6)   When a draft of an order is laid, the code to which it relates must also be laid.

(7) No draft of an order may be laid until the consultation required by subsection (3) has taken place.

(8) An order bringing a code into operation may include transitional or saving provisions."

4   After subsection (10) of section 71 insert—   5

"(11) The reference in subsection (2) to powers and duties conferred by or under Part 1 of the Communications Data Act 2012 does not include a reference to any such powers and duties which are conferred on the Secretary of State."

5   In the heading to section 71, the words "and revision" are repealed.   10

6   After section 71 insert—

"71A Revision of codes of practice

(1) The Secretary of State may from time to time revise the whole or part of a code of practice issued under section 71.

(2) Before issuing any revision of a code the Secretary of State must—   15
    (a) prepare and publish a draft, and
    (b) consider any representations made about it,
    and may modify the draft.

(3) A revision of a code does not come into operation until the Secretary of State by order so provides.   20

(4) An order bringing a revision of a code into operation must be laid before Parliament if the order has been made without a draft having been so laid and approved by a resolution of each House of Parliament.

(5) When an order or draft of an order is laid, the revision of a code to 25
    which it relates must also be laid.

(6) No order or draft of an order may be laid until the consultation required by subsection (2) has taken place.

(7) An order bringing a revision of a code into operation may include transitional or saving provisions."   30

7   In section 72 (effect of codes of practice: functions of relevant Commissioners)—
    (a) in subsection (4)(c) after "this Act" insert "or the Communications Data Act 2012", and
    (b) in subsection (5) after "Intelligence Services Commissioner" insert ", 35
         the Information Commissioner".

Schedule 4: Consequential Provision

148.   Schedule 4 makes consequential amendments to other enactments.

SCHEDULE 4 Section 31(1)

CONSEQUENTIAL PROVISION

PART 1

GENERAL CONSEQUENTIAL PROVISION

Northern Ireland Act 1998 (c. 47) 5

1 (1) Paragraph 9(1) of Schedule 3 to the Northern Ireland Act 1998 (reserved matters) is amended as follows.

   (2) After "following matters—" insert—

      "(za) the subject matter of Part 2 of the Communications Data Act 2012 so far as relating to— 10

         (i) the prevention or detection of crime (within the meaning of that Part of that Act), or

         (ii) the prevention of disorder;".

   (3) In paragraph (a)(ii), paragraph (aa) and the word "and" at the end of paragraph (aa) are repealed. 15

Regulation of Investigatory Powers Act 2000 (c. 23)

2 The Regulation of Investigatory Powers Act 2000 is amended as follows.

3 In section 2 (meaning and location of "interception" etc.)—

   (a) in subsection (9), at the end of paragraph (c) (and before "and"), insert— 20

      "(ca) any data identifying, or purporting to identify, the time at which an event relating to the communication occurs,", and

   (b) in subsection (10) for "means", where it appears for the second time, substitute "includes". 25

4 In section 20 (interception: interpretation), in the definition of "related communications data", for "of Chapter II of this Part" substitute "given by section 28 of the Communications Data Act 2012 (communications data: interpretation)".

5 Sections 21 to 25 (acquisition and disclosure of communications data) are 30 repealed.

6 The following provisions are repealed (repeals consequential on repeal of sections 21 to 25)—

   (a) section 57(2)(b),

   (b) in section 58(1)— 35

      (i) paragraphs (g) and (h), and

      (ii) in paragraph (j), the text ", (h)",

   (c) section 65(5)(c) and (8)(b), and

   (d) in section 68(7)—

      (i) paragraphs (g) and (h), and 40

      (ii) in paragraph (n), the text ", (h)".

7   In section 49(1)(c) (notices requiring disclosure) for the words from "an authorisation" to "section 22(4)" substitute "virtue of an authorisation under section 9 or 19 of the Communications Data Act 2012 or Part 2 of this Act".

8   In section 77A (procedure for order of sheriff under section 23A or 32A: Scotland)—   5

    (a)   in the heading for "23A or 32A" substitute "32A of this Act or section 11 of the Communications Data Act 2012",

    (b)   in subsection (1) for "23A or 32A" substitute "32A of this Act or section 11 of the Communications Data Act 2012", and

    (c)   in subsection (3) for "sections 23B and 32B and this section" 10 substitute "section 32B and this section of this Act and section 11 of the Communications Data Act 2012".

9   In section 77B (procedure for order of district judge under section 23A or 32A: Northern Ireland)—

    (a)   in the heading for "23A or 32A" substitute "32A of this Act or section 15 11 of the Communications Data Act 2012",

    (b)   in subsection (1) for "23A or 32A" substitute "32A of this Act or section 11 of the Communications Data Act 2012", and

    (c)   in subsection (4)—

        (i)   for "23A or 32A" substitute "32A of this Act or section 11 of 20 the Communications Data Act 2012", and

        (ii)   for "sections 23B and 32B and any order made under this section" substitute "section 32B of this Act, any order made under this section, and section 11 of the Communications Data Act 2012".   25

10   In section 78(3)(a) (orders subject to negative instrument procedure) the words "22(9), 23A(6), 25(5)," are repealed.

11   In section 81(9) (interpretation), the word "23A(7)(b)," is repealed.

Anti-terrorism, Crime and Security Act 2001 (c. 24)

12   Part 11 of the Anti-terrorism, Crime and Security Act 2001 (retention of 30 communications data) is repealed.

Wireless Telegraphy Act 2006 (c. 36)

13   (1)   Section 49 of the Wireless Telegraphy Act 2006 (interception authorities) is amended as follows.

    (2)   In subsection (2)—   35

        (a)   paragraph (c) and the word "or" at the end of paragraph (c) are repealed, and

        (b)   after paragraph (d) insert "; or

            (e)   conduct that is capable of being authorised by virtue of an authorisation under Part 2 of the 40 Communications Data Act 2012 (regulatory regime for obtaining communications data)."

    (3)   In subsection (10)—

        (a)   in the opening words, for "Chapter 2 of Part 1 of the Regulation of Investigatory Powers Act 2000 (c 23) or under Part 2 of that Act" 45

substitute "Part 2 of the Regulation of Investigatory Powers Act 2000 or by virtue of an authorisation under Part 2 of the Communications Data Act 2012", and

(b)   in paragraphs (a) and (b), the words "that Chapter or" are repealed.

(4) In subsection (11), after "Part 1 or 2 of the Regulation of Investigatory 5 Powers Act 2000" insert "or Part 2 of the Communications Data Act 2012".

PART 2

MINOR CONSEQUENTIAL REPEALS AND REVOCATIONS

Title	Extent of repeal or revocation	
Serious Organised Crime and Police Act 2005 (c. 15)	In Schedule 4, paragraph 135.	10
Serious Crime Act 2007 (c. 27)	In Schedule 12, paragraphs 7 and 8.	
Police, Public Order and Criminal Justice (Scotland) Act 2006 (Consequential Provisions and Modifications) Order 2007 (S.I. 2007/1098)	In the Schedule, paragraph 4(5).	15
Policing and Crime Act 2009 (c. 26)	Section 7. Part 2 of Schedule 7.	20
Protection of Freedoms Act 2012 (c. 9)	Section 37. In Schedule 9, paragraphs 7, 8, 10, 13 and 16(b)(i) (and the word "and" at the end of paragraph 16(b)(i)).	

COMMENCEMENT

149.   The provisions in clauses 29, 30, 31(2) and (3), 32 and 33 (general) come into force on Royal Assent.

150.   All other provisions will be brought into force by means of commencement orders made by the Secretary of State.

FINANCIAL EFFECTS OF THE BILL

151.   The programme to ensure the availability of communications data by telecommunications operators and for the obtaining of such data by law enforcement agencies and relevant public authorities, enabled by Parts 1 and 2 of the Bill, is estimated to lead to an increase in public expenditure of up to £1.8 billion over 10 years from 2011/12. Benefits from this investment are estimated to be £5 – 6.2 billion over the same period.

EFFECTS OF THE BILL ON PUBLIC SECTOR MANPOWER

152.   As of 1 April 2012 the Home Office Communications Capabilities Development Programme, which is responsible for the delivery of the activity referred to above, has 120 staff (full time equivalents). This is envisaged to fall to around 40 staff over a 10 year period when the new framework will be fully in place.

SUMMARY OF IMPACT ASSESSMENTS

153.   The Bill is accompanied by an impact assessment and privacy impact assessment. These are available on the Home Office website.

EUROPEAN CONVENTION FOR HUMAN RIGHTS

154.   The Government has published a separate ECHR memorandum with its assessment of the compatibility of the Bill's provisions with the Convention rights; the memorandum is available on the Home Office website.

ANNEX

Examples of communications data

155.   There are three primary types of communications data as defined in this Bill:

- *Subscriber Data* – Subscriber data is information held or obtained by a provider in relation to persons to whom the service is provided by that provider. Those persons will include people who are subscribers to a communications service without necessarily using that service and persons who use a communications service without necessarily subscribing to it. Examples of subscriber information include:

    – 'Subscriber checks' (also known as 'reverse look ups') such as "who is the subscriber of phone number 012 345 6789?", "who is the account holder of e-mail account xyz@xyz.anyisp.co.uk?" or "who is entitled to post to web space www.xyz.anyisp.co.uk?";
    – Subscribers' or account holders' account information, including names and addresses for installation, and billing including payment method(s), details of payments;

- information about the connection, disconnection and reconnection of services which the subscriber or account holder is allocated or has subscribed to (or may have subscribed to) including conference calling, call messaging, call waiting and call barring telecommunications services;
- information about the provision to a subscriber or account holder of forwarding/ redirection services;
- information about apparatus used by, or made available to, the subscriber or account holder, including the manufacturer, model, serial numbers and apparatus codes.
- information provided by a subscriber or account holder to a provider, such as demographic information or sign-up data (to the extent that information, such as a password, giving access to the content of any stored communications is not disclosed).

- *Use data* – Use data is information about the use made by any person of a postal or telecommunications service. Examples of use data may include:

  - itemised telephone call records (numbers called);
  - itemised records of connections to internet services;
  - itemised timing and duration of service usage (calls and/or connections);
  - information about amounts of data downloaded and/or uploaded;
  - information about the use made of services which the user is allocated or has subscribed to (or may have subscribed to) including conference calling, call messaging, call waiting and call barring telecommunications services;
  - information about the use of forwarding/redirection services;
  - information about selection of preferential numbers or discount calls;

- *Traffic Data*: Traffic data is data that is comprised in or attached to a communication for the purpose of transmitting the communication. Examples of traffic data may include:

  - information tracing the origin or destination of a communication that is in transmission;
  - information identifying the location of equipment when a communication is or has been made or received (such as the location of a mobile phone);
  - information identifying the sender and recipient (including copy recipients) of a communication from data comprised in or attached to the communication;
  - routing information identifying equipment through which a communication is or has been transmitted (for example, dynamic IP address allocation, file transfer logs and e-mail headers – to the extent that content of a communication, such as the subject line of an e-mail, is not disclosed);
  - anything, such as addresses or markings, written on the outside of a postal item (such as a letter, packet or parcel) that is in transmission;
  - online tracking of communications (including postal items and parcels).

DRAFT COMMUNICATIONS DATA BILL

EUROPEAN CONVENTION ON HUMAN RIGHTS

MEMORANDUM BY THE HOME OFFICE

1. This memorandum addresses issues arising under the European Convention on Human Rights ("ECHR") in relation to the draft Communications Data Bill. The Government is satisfied that, in the event that the Bill is introduced into Parliament, the responsible Minister could make a statement under section 19(1)(a) of the Human Rights Act 1998 that, in his or her view, the provisions of the Bill are compatible with the Convention rights.

Overview

2. Part 1 of the Bill makes provision for ensuring or facilitating that communications data is available to be obtained from telecommunications operators by relevant public authorities under Part 2.

3. Clause 1 permits the Secretary of State, by order, to provide, in particular, for the obtaining, processing and retention of communications data by telecommunications operators to ensure the availability of such data. The intention is that the clause 1 power will be exercised, amongst other things, to impose requirements on operators to:

   - generate all necessary communications data for the services or systems they provide;
   - collect necessary communications data, where such data is available but not retained;
   - retain such data safely and securely;
   - process the retained data to facilitate the efficient and effective obtaining of the data by public authorities;
   - undertake testing of their internal systems;
   - co-operate with the Secretary of State or other specified persons to ensure the availability of communications data.

4. Clauses 2 to 6 make express provision for safeguards in relation to Part 1. These safeguards include requirements relating to consultation, data security and integrity, retention periods, access to the data and destruction of the data at the end of the retention period. Clause 7 makes further provision for procedural safeguards, including the reference of notices to the Technical Advisory Board.

5. Part 2 of the Bill replaces the provisions in Chapter 2 of Part 1 of the Regulation of Investigatory Powers Act 2000 ("RIPA") for acquiring communications data (those provisions are repealed by paragraph 5 of Schedule 4). Chapter 2 of Part 1 of RIPA was enacted in order to provide public authorities with a human rights compliant framework for acquiring

communications data. The new scheme in Part 2 of the Bill preserves the essential elements of this framework. In particular, the substantive protections of Article 8 will continue to be guaranteed by the express terms of Part 2 which only permit the exercise of the relevant powers if the tests of necessity, proportionality and legitimate aim are satisfied.

6. Clause 14 makes provision for the Secretary of State to establish new filtering arrangements for facilitating the lawful, efficient and effective obtaining of communications data pursuant to an authorisation. The filtering arrangements created by the Bill are, in summary, a system for automatically filtering communications data obtained from operators in accordance with predetermined rules in order to provide public authorities with the subset of data relevant to their request. The filtering arrangements created by the Bill are described in more detail in the Explanatory Notes for clauses 14-16.

7. Part 3 of the Bill confers scrutiny functions relating to the new legislative scheme on the Interception of Communications Commissioner, the Information Commissioner and the Investigatory Powers Tribunal, and makes provision about codes of practice.

Article 8

Generally

8. It is well established that mail, telephone and email communications are covered by the notion of private life and correspondence in Article 8(1). The case of *Malone v UK* (1984) 7 EHRR 14 (paragraphs 83 to 88) provides some limited guidance on the application of Article 8 to State activities concerning communications data:

> *".... a meter check printer registers information that a supplier of a telephone service may in principle legitimately obtain, notably in order to ensure that the subscriber is correctly charged or to investigate complaints or possible abuses of the service. By its very nature, metering is therefore to be distinguished from interception of communications, which is undesirable and illegitimate in a democratic society unless justified. The Court does not accept, however, that the use of data obtained from metering, whatever the circumstances and purposes, cannot give rise to an issue under Article 8. The records of metering contain information, in particular the numbers dialled, which is an integral element in the communications made by telephone. Consequently, release of that information to the police without the consent of the subscriber also amounts, in the opinion of the Court, to an interference with a right guaranteed by Article 8."*

9. The primary function of Article 8 is to impose negative obligations on States: States cannot interfere with Article 8(1) rights save where such interferences can be justified under Article 8(2). There can be no violation of this negative obligation by the actions of private persons. The negative

obligation does not therefore need to be considered unless the person whose actions are being considered is a public authority within the meaning of section 6(3) of the Human Rights Act 1998 ("the HRA").

10. However, Article 8 may also impose certain positive obligations on States to adopt measures designed to secure respect for private life even as between private persons. It follows that there may be a breach of such positive obligations if the State requires private persons to interfere excessively with the privacy of others, or in the absence of adequate safeguards[1].

11. Part 1 of the Bill will enable the Secretary of State to impose requirements and restrictions on telecommunications operators to obtain, process and retain communications data. Part 1 is an essential component of the Government's strategy to maintain existing communications data capabilities in light of ongoing developments in telecommunications technology. The ability of law enforcement and intelligence agencies to obtain communications data is vital in protecting national security, preventing and detecting crime and protecting the public[2]. Communications data is used not only as evidence in court, but also to eliminate people from law enforcement investigations. It can be used to prove a person's innocence as well as his or her guilt. This also explains why it is not possible to simply retain the communications data of those who have committed a crime. For example, it would not be possible to retain the communications data of criminals without being aware in advance of the crimes they were planning to commit (such as the phone calls between conspirators before a bank robbery that are later used to prove their association in court). In addition, communications data is often used to piece together the last movements of a victim of crime. Part 1 will ensure that all communications data of this sort continues to be available to be obtained by the law enforcement and intelligence agencies and other relevant public authorities.

12. Although telecommunications operators are unlikely to qualify as public authorities for the purposes of the HRA in relation to Part 1, Article 8 may impose positive obligations upon the State as a whole so as to regulate the performance of the duties imposed on operators under Part 1 and, in particular, to ensure that there are appropriate safeguards in place.

13. In so far as any relevant positive obligation arises, Part 1 must be assessed together with all other relevant measures that are in place to

---

[1] See e.g., *Botta v Italy* (1998) 26 EHRR 241, at para. 33.
[2] See e.g., K.U. v Finland [2008] ECHR 2872/02, at para. 49 ("....Although freedom of expression and confidentiality of communications are primary considerations and users of telecommunications and Internet services must have a guarantee that their own privacy and freedom of expression will be respected, such guarantee cannot be absolute and must yield on occasion to other legitimate imperatives, such as the prevention of disorder or crime or the protection of the rights and freedoms of others. ...It is nonetheless the task of the legislator to provide the framework for reconciling the various claims which compete for protection in this context."

respect and protect privacy[3]. Part 1 of the Bill contains an extensive range of safeguards against abuse to ensure that operators are subject to all the obligations necessary to secure respect for the private life of individual telecommunications users. The safeguards mentioned in paragraph 21 below are also relevant in this context by way of ensuring that there are "adequate and effective guarantees against abuse" as regards the interferences consequent upon relevant public authorities gaining access to retained communications data. Further, the fact that the data will be retained by individual telecommunications operators rather than by Government is an additional safeguard against abuse. In practice, it is likely that a clause 1 order will provide for more specific requirements or restrictions to be imposed on individual telecommunications operators or other persons by notice of the Secretary of State. These requirements or restrictions will relate to particular systems and services provided by an operator, and will impose requirements with respect to particular descriptions of data. The Government's implementation strategy will be based, in the first instance, on collaboration with individual operators to ensure the availability, in relation to that operator's systems or services, of the data that is operationally necessary for relevant public authorities to obtain. The Secretary of State is obliged by virtue of clause 2 to consult operators before making any such order under clause 1, and an operator may refer the notice imposing any requirement or restriction to the Technical Advisory Board in accordance with clause 7(2).

14. The other key safeguards in Part 1 are as follows:

(i) Clause 3 makes provision for the security and integrity of communications data held by operators;

(ii) A maximum retention period of 12 months is specified in clause 4 (although that period may be extended if data is required for legal proceedings);

(iii) Operators must destroy the data at the end of the retention period in accordance with clause 6;

(iv) Clause 5 imposes restrictions on access to retained data:

- Subsection (1) prohibits the disclosure of communications data held by an operator except in accordance with the provisions of Part 2 or otherwise as authorised by law;

- Subsection (2) provides that an operator must put in place adequate security systems governing access to the data to protect against any disclosure of a kind which does not fall within subsection (1).

---

[3] See *Von Hannover v. Germany* (2004) 40 EHRR 1.

(v) Part 1 contains other safeguards in relation to orders under clause 1 relating to consultation and procedural requirements, and the reference of certain notices to the Technical Advisory Board (established by section 13 of RIPA);

(vi) The Information Commissioner and the Interception of Communications Commissioner have new powers to oversee this aspect of the statutory scheme by virtue of clause 22.

15. Accordingly, the Government considers that the safeguards provided by Part 1 of the Bill are sufficient to discharge any positive obligations that Article 8 might impose in relation to the activities of telecommunications operators as private persons being required to interfere with the privacy rights of communications users.

Article 8(1)

16. It follows from *Malone* that the transfer of communications data from a telecommunications operator to a public authority will in general interfere with Article 8(1) rights. The transfer of communications data from one public authority to another will also give rise to a distinct interference with Article 8(1) requiring separate justification under Article 8(2).

17. The Article 8(1) interferences which will need to be capable of justification under Article 8(2) are accordingly: (i) the obtaining of communications data by public authorities pursuant to an authorisation; and (ii) the obtaining, processing and disclosure of communications data by the filtering arrangements in pursuance of an authorisation.

Article 8(2)

18. Article 8(2) sets out the grounds on which interferences with the protected rights may be justified. Justification of an interference under Article 8(2) requires that the interference in question is: (i) "in accordance with the law", (ii) for a legitimate aim (or aims) and (iii) proportionate, having regard to the aim (or aims) at issue.

19. The interferences will be in accordance with the law because there will be clear provision in primary legislation governing (a) the obtaining of communications data by relevant public authorities and (b) the obtaining, processing and disclosure of that communications data by the filtering arrangements. These provisions are formulated with sufficient precision to enable a person to know in what circumstances and to what extent the powers can be exercised.

20. The interferences with Convention rights caused by the obtaining of communications data by public authorities will be in pursuit of a legitimate aim. An authorisation may only be granted if a designated senior officer of a relevant public authority believes that it is necessary to obtain the data for a permitted purpose, and that the conduct authorised is proportionate

to what is sought to be achieved by obtaining the data. The permitted purposes pursue the legitimate aims set out in clause 9(6), namely:

a) in the interests of national security,
b) for the purpose of preventing or detecting crime or of preventing disorder,
c) for the purpose of preventing or detecting any conduct in respect of which a penalty may be imposed under section 123 or 129 of the Financial Services and Markets Act 2000 (civil penalties for market abuse),
d) in the interests of the economic well-being of the United Kingdom,
e) in the interests of public safety,
f) for the purpose of protecting public health,
g) for the purpose of assessing or collecting any tax, duty, levy or other imposition, contribution or charge payable to a government department,
h) for the purpose, in an emergency, of preventing death or injury or any damage to a person's physical or mental health, or of mitigating any injury or damage to a person's physical or mental health,
i) to assist investigations into alleged miscarriages of justice, or
j) where a person ("P") has died or is unable to identify themselves because of a physical or mental condition-
   i. to assist in identifying P, or
   ii. to obtain information about P's next of kin or other persons connected with P or about the reason for P's death or condition.

21. The interferences with these rights will also be proportionate for the reasons set out below, including the extensive range of safeguards and restrictions against abuse:

(i) The European Court of Human Rights has accepted that States should be accorded a wide margin of appreciation in this area (see *Weber and Saravia v. Germany* (2008) 46 EHRR SE5, at paragraph 106), and it is clear from *Malone* that the Court considers the acquisition of communications data to be a less serious infringement of privacy rights than the interception of communications;

(ii) It is essential that the UK is able to obtain communications data in the interests of national security and the prevention and detection of crime;

(iii) The reduction in the availability of communications data will have extremely serious consequences for the UK. The provisions in the Bill are an essential component of the long term strategy necessary to mitigate the reduction in capabilities caused by the decline in the availability of communications data, and to ensure that public authorities continue to have sufficient access to communications data to perform their duties and to support intelligence agency and law enforcement activities;

(iv) Part 2 makes three substantive improvements to the provisions governing the acquisition of communications data in order to enhance the Article 8 compatibility of the scheme as a whole;

- First, clause 9, in conjunction with the new duty in clause 13(1), enhances the ability of the senior designated officer to assess the Article 8(1) interferences arising from the processing of data by operators, and therefore to determine whether, in any case, the officer believes that the tests of necessity and proportionality are met;

- Secondly, the filtering arrangements will minimise the interference with Article 8(1) rights, to which requests for communications data in an Internet environment will necessarily give rise. In particular, any necessary pre-processing and collation of communications data will occur before the data is disclosed to the relevant public authority without the need for human intervention. The filtering arrangements will only ever disclose the filtered, proportionate subset of requested data to the relevant public authority. The fact that the most intrusive aspects of the conduct necessary to obtain the data will be automated by the filtering arrangements without the need for human intervention or control, and will be invisible to the public authority who requested the data, will ensure that the Article 8(1) interferences associated with the obtaining, processing and disclosure of communications data are minimised, and the Article 8 compatibility of the scheme as a whole is enhanced;

- Thirdly, clause 24 restricts the use of general information powers by public authorities to secure the disclosure by telecommunications operators of communications data without the consent of the operator. Clause 24 therefore ensures that operators are not required by law to obtain and disclose communications data other than in cases where the relevant statutory framework expressly guarantees the substantive protections of Article 8 and Directive 2002/58/EC (Directive on privacy and electronic communications);

(v) Part 2 provides an extensive range of additional safeguards and restrictions. The granting of authorisations will be restricted to those cases where the communications data is required for the purposes of a specific investigation or a specific operation or for the purposes of testing, maintaining or developing equipment, systems or other capabilities relating to the availability or obtaining of communications data. Orders made under clause 17 will, as at present, place significant restrictions on the authorisations that may be granted by a designated senior officer with a specified public authority and on the circumstances in which, or the purposes for which, such authorisations may be granted by the officer;

(vi) There will be restrictions imposed by secondary legislation on the relevant public authorities that may use the filtering arrangements, the permitted purposes in clause 9 for which the filtering arrangements may be used, and the types of data that may be processed, by means of the filtering arrangements;

(vii) The Information Commissioner and the Interception of Communications Commissioner will have new powers of oversight as regards the exercise and performance of the powers and duties conferred and imposed by the Bill;

(viii) The Investigatory Powers Tribunal will have jurisdiction to entertain claims or complaints (whether brought under the HRA or otherwise) in relation to the operation of the Bill; and

(ix) A new code of practice issued under section 71 of RIPA will impose certain additional practical safeguards relating to matters such as record-keeping and the reporting of errors.

22. Accordingly, the Government considers the Bill is compatible with Article 8.

Home Office
June 2012

DRAFT COMMUNICATIONS DATA BILL

DELEGATED POWERS

MEMORANDUM BY THE HOME OFFICE

Introduction

1. This Memorandum identifies the provisions of the draft Communications Data Bill which confers powers to make delegated legislation, and explains in each case why the power has been taken and the nature of, and reason for, the procedure selected.

2. The Bill makes updated provision for ensuring the availability of communications data and for the obtaining of such data by relevant public authorities including law enforcement and other agencies.

PART 1: ENSURING OR FACILITATING AVAILABILITY OF COMMUNICATIONS DATA

Clause 1(1): Power to ensure or facilitate availability of data.

Power conferred on: *Secretary of State*

Power exercisable by: *Order made by statutory instrument*

Parliamentary procedure: *Affirmative resolution*

3. Part 1 of the Bill is founded on the power in clause 1 for the Secretary of State, by order, to ensure or otherwise facilitate the availability of communications data from telecommunications operators by relevant public authorities in accordance with Part 2. The power in clause 1 sets the parameters for Part 1 and explains the purposes for which the power may be exercised. Clause 1(2)(a) sets out the main ways in which it is expected that the clause 1 power will be exercised. It is anticipated that an order under clause 1 will, amongst other things, impose requirements on operators to:

   - generate all necessary communications data for the services or systems they provide;
   - collect necessary communications data, where such data is available but not retained;
   - retain such data safely and securely;
   - process the retained data to facilitate the efficient and effective obtaining of the data by public authorities;
   - undertake testing of their internal systems; and

- co-operate with the Secretary of State or other specified persons to ensure the availability of communications data.

4. The clause 1 order will also provide for more specific requirements or restrictions to be imposed on individual telecommunications operators or other persons by notice of the Secretary of State. In practice, it is expected that any requirements or restrictions imposed by virtue of a notice will relate to particular systems and services, or classes of systems and services, provided by an operator, and will impose requirements with respect to particular descriptions of data. The expectation is that notices will therefore be individually tailored to each system or service (or class of system or service) in respect of which there is an operational need for communications data to be available from an operator. The notices will describe, by reference to each service and system, the description of data which must be retained, where that data should be stored and, if necessary, how the data should be generated and processed.

5. Clauses 2 to 7 make express provision for safeguards in relation to Part 1. These safeguards include, by virtue of clauses 3 to 6, mandatory obligations on telecommunications operators who hold communications data by virtue of this Part relating to data security and integrity, retention periods, access to the data and destruction of the data at the end of the retention period. Clause 2 imposes consultation requirements on the Secretary of State and clause 7 makes provision for further procedural safeguards, including the referral of notices to the Technical Advisory Board (established by section 13 of RIPA).

6. The clause 1 power is required in order to provide the flexibility necessary to ensure the availability of communications data against the backdrop of a continuously evolving communications environment. Communications services are volatile and change rapidly in response to commercial drivers and other technological innovations. Services are increasingly delivered by a variety of commercial and technical relationships which means that communications data is fragmented and dispersed amongst numerous companies. No single solution or implementation strategy will therefore be capable of responding to all future technological developments or market innovations, or of satisfying the range of operational requirements of the law enforcement and intelligence agencies and other public authorities. Any sustainable solution will need to be capable of accommodating a range of different implementation models over time in order to ensure the availability of communications data.

7. Clause 1 accordingly provides the flexibility necessary to deal with the complexity of the domestic and global telecommunications market, and to respond to future evolutions in technology. Any order under clause 1 will enable provision to be made to ensure the availability of communications data in the light of these developments depending on the most appropriate implementation model at any particular time.

Given the significant implications for telecommunications operators and the importance of the public policy issues addressed by clause 1, orders under this clause will be subject to the affirmative resolution procedure (see clause 29(2)(a)). This will ensure that Parliament is able to debate and approve the proposed exercise of the power and to retain the necessary degree of oversight and control over the use of the power. The requirements imposed on telecommunications operators by virtue of an order made under clause 1 will sit alongside the requirements imposed by the EU Data Retention Directive transposed into UK law by the Data Retention (EU Directive) Regulations 2009 (S.I. 2009/859).

PART 2: REGULATORY REGIME FOR OBTAINING DATA

Clause 9(7): Power to add to or restrict the purposes for which communications data may be obtained.

Power conferred on: *Secretary of State*

Power exercisable by: *Order made by statutory instrument*

Parliamentary procedure: *Affirmative resolution*

8. Clause 9(6) sets out the permitted purposes for which communications data may be acquired under Part 2. The permitted purposes in subsection (6) mirror the legitimate aims in Article 8(2) ECHR, but deliberately omit "the protection of morals" and "protecting the rights and freedoms of others".

9. Subsection (7) permits the Secretary of State to add to or restrict the permitted purposes. This power will enable additional purposes falling within the scope of the "missing" Article 8(2) purposes to be added to subsection (6), and will enable restrictions to be imposed on the existing purposes. The power to add to the permitted purposes in subsection (6) is necessary to ensure that public authorities who may at some time in the future need to obtain communications data for the protection of morals or to protect the rights and freedoms of others can be given the powers they need to carry out their functions. Any new purposes of this nature will be custom made for the public authority in issue. Subsection (7) replicates a similar power in section 25 of the Regulation of Investigatory Powers Act 2000 (see S.I. 2010/480).

10. The power to add purposes by order is particularly important in the light of clause 24 which restricts the use of general information powers by public authorities to secure the disclosure by operators of communications data without the consent of the operator. In the absence of the power in clause 9(7), new or existing bodies who need to acquire communications data for purposes falling within the missing Article 8(2) purposes will be unable to do so. Such bodies may accordingly be prevented from carrying out their statutory functions.

11. Given that the permitted purposes for which communications data may be acquired are set out on the face of the Bill, the Government considers that any extension or modification of such purposes should be subject to debate and prior approval by both Houses through the affirmative procedure (which applies by virtue of clause 29(2)(a)).

Clause 11: Judicial approval for certain authorisations–

i.   **Subsections (4)(a)(iii) and (4)(b)(iii) – Power to prescribe further conditions that must be satisfied for the purpose of judicial approval of local authority authorisation.**
ii. **Subsection (4)(c) – Power to prescribe conditions that must be satisfied for the purpose of judicial approval of authorisation by other "relevant person".**
iii. **Subsection (6), paragraph (c) of definition of "relevant person" - Power to prescribe further "relevant persons".**

Powers conferred on: *Secretary of State*

Exercisable by: *Orders made by statutory instrument*

Parliamentary procedure: *(i) Negative resolution; (ii) Negative resolution; (iii) Affirmative resolution*

12. Clause 11 provides that local authorities may only obtain and disclose communications data under Part 2 of the Bill if the local authority's authorisation has itself been approved by a relevant judicial authority (a magistrate or, in Scotland, a sheriff). The clause provides that: (i) the Secretary of State may by order prescribe additional conditions which the judicial authority must be satisfied were met before approving a local authority authorisation; (ii) with respect to judicial approval of authorisations by public authorities other than local authorities, the Secretary of State may by order prescribe the conditions which the judicial authority must be satisfied were met; and (iii) the Secretary of State may by order provide that other public authorities or types of authorisations by other public authorities should be subject to the judicial approval process.

13. Under subsection (3) the relevant judicial authority may approve a local authority authorisation where it is satisfied that obtaining the communications data was and remains proportionate and necessary on specified grounds. The judicial authority must also be satisfied that, when the authorisation or renewal was granted, the prescribed relevant conditions were satisfied.

14. The relevant conditions which apply to authorisations granted or given by local authorities are set out in clause 11(4). They are that the individual from the local authority who granted the authorisation was

designated to do so, and that the grant was not in breach of any restrictions or prohibition imposed by clause 17. That clause allows the Secretary of State by order to impose restrictions on the individuals that may grant an authorisation and on the circumstances in which or purposes for which the authorisation may be given.

15. The order-making powers in this clause mirror those in section 23A of RIPA, as inserted by section 37 of the Protection of Freedoms Act 2012.

i.   **Subsections (4)(a)(iii) and (4)(b)(iii) – Power to prescribe further conditions that must be satisfied for the purpose of judicial approval of local authority authorisation.**

16. Order-making powers are provided in subsection (4)(a)(iii) (England and Wales and Scotland) and subsection (4)(b)(iii) (Northern Ireland). The purpose of these orders is to allow the Secretary of State to specify any further conditions that must be satisfied in respect of the grant or renewal of authorisations or the giving of notices by local authorities.

17. The key relevant conditions that the judicial authority must be satisfied were met before granting approval are set out in subsection (4)(a)(i) and (ii) and (4)(b)(i) and (ii). These reflect most of the statutory conditions which must be met if the local authority is to grant the authorisation. Part 2, however, specifies a number of other conditions which also apply to authorisations for communications data, for example, they must be granted in writing (clause 10(5)).

18. It would be cumbersome to set out in the primary legislation all of the statutory conditions which potentially apply to the underlying authorisation and to require the magistrate to be satisfied that each has been met before granting the approval. To do so might appear to place equal emphasis on the conditions. Instead, the key conditions which the magistrate must be satisfied were met are set out in subsection (4). The order-making power then allows the Secretary of State to specify any additional conditions that the magistrate must be satisfied were met as a threshold for granting judicial approval.

19. It is not necessary for the Secretary of State to exercise these order-making powers so that the judicial approval mechanism can operate. There is already a residual discretion for the magistrate or sheriff to decline to give approval to the authorisation under subsection (3). Thus it would be possible for the judicial authority to refuse to approve the authorisation even where it was satisfied that the conditions specified in subsection (4)(a)(i) and (ii) or (4)(b)(i) and (ii) were met.

20. The order-making powers in subsection (4) are, by virtue of clause 29(3)(a), subject to the negative procedure. This is considered appropriate as the orders will be used only to set out any additional

conditions that the judicial authority must be satisfied have been met. The order will not affect the statutory conditions which attach to the underlying authorisation which will still have to be met.

ii. **Subsection (4)(c) – Power to prescribe conditions that must be satisfied for the purpose of judicial approval of authorisation by other "relevant person".**

21. The powers in subsections (4)(c) allow the Secretary of State to prescribe the relevant conditions which the judicial authority must be satisfied were met in relation to an authorisation made by any other public authority other than a local authority. This will allow the Secretary of State to prescribe all relevant conditions when additional authorisations or grants or renewals are subjected to the judicial approval process.

22. This order-making power is, by virtue of clause 29(3)(a), subject to the negative procedure. This is considered appropriate as the orders will be used only to set out those relevant conditions the judicial authority must be satisfied are met before granting approval. The order will not affect the statutory conditions which attach to the underlying authorisation or notice.

iii. **Subsection (6), paragraph (c) of definition of "relevant person" – Power to prescribe further "relevant persons".**

23. This power effectively provides that the Secretary of State may prescribe additional public authorities or descriptions of authorisations made by other public authorities to which the judicial approval process may be applied. This will allow the Secretary of State to apply the judicial approval process to authorisations made by public authorities other than local authorities.

24. This order-making power is, by virtue of clause 29(2)(a), subject to the affirmative procedure. Given that any such order would achieve the effect that additional public authorities would be subjected to (or, potentially, removed from) the judicial approval procedure, it is considered appropriate that any order made under these provisions should be debated and approved by both Houses.

Clause 12(5): Power to provide that the duty imposed on a designated senior officer to cancel an authorisation may be performed by another person.

Power conferred on:　　　　*Secretary of State*

Power exercisable by:　　　　*Regulations made by statutory instrument*

Parliamentary procedure:　　　　*Negative resolution*

25. Clause 12 makes provision for the duration and cancellation of authorisations under clause 9. A designated senior officer who has granted an authorisation under clause 9 must, by virtue of clause 12(4), cancel the authorisation if satisfied that the position is no longer as mentioned in clause 9(1)(a), (b) and (c).

26. Clause 12(5) provides a regulation-making power to cater for the possibility that the person on whom the subsection (4) duty is to be performed is no longer available to perform it. In particular, subsection (6) provides that the regulations may provide for the person on whom the duty is to fall to be a person appointed by the regulations. Clause 12(5) mirrors the equivalent power in section 23(9) of RIPA.

27. The negative procedure (which applies by virtue of clause 29(3)(a)) provides the appropriate level of parliamentary control for a power of this nature.

Clause 17(1): Power to impose restrictions on the granting of authorisations.

Power conferred on: *Secretary of State*

Power exercisable by: *Order made by statutory instrument*

Parliamentary procedure: *Affirmative resolution*

28. Clause 17 permits the Secretary of State, by order, to impose restrictions on the granting of authorisations by designated senior officers.

29. By clause 17(3) such orders will, as at present, place significant restrictions on the authorisations that may be granted by a designated senior officer with a specified public authority, and on the circumstances in which, or the purposes for which, such authorisations may be granted by the officer. These restrictions will be assessed on a case by case basis by reference to each relevant public authority and may, in particular, restrict the types of communications data which may be obtained by particular bodies, and the permitted purposes for which those bodies may obtain the data. Equivalent provision is made in section 25(3) of RIPA (see S.I. 2010/480).

30. By clause 17(4), new restrictions will also be imposed, as regards authorisations, on the public authorities that may use the filtering arrangements, the permitted purposes for which the arrangements may be used, and the data that may be processed by means of the filtering arrangements.

31. Clause 17 constitutes an important component of the safeguards provided by Part 2. As there will be a significant level of Parliamentary

interest in the nature and extent of the restrictions imposed, the affirmative resolution procedure (which is applied by clause 29(2)(a)) is considered appropriate for this power.

Clause 20(1) and (2): Power to designate a public authority to exercise functions under clauses 14 to 16.

Power conferred on: *Secretary of State*

Power exercisable by: *Order made by statutory instrument*

Parliamentary procedure: *Affirmative resolution*

32. Clause 14 makes provision for the Secretary of State to establish, maintain and operate filtering arrangements for facilitating the obtaining of communications data by relevant public authorities. The filtering arrangements created by the Bill are, in summary, a system for automatically filtering communications data obtained from operators in accordance with predetermined rules in order to provide public authorities with the subset of data relevant to their request. The wider set of data obtained by the filtering arrangements will be immediately deleted at the point the subset of relevant data is disclosed to the public authority making the request. Clause 16 imposes further duties on the Secretary of State in connection with the operation of the filtering arrangements. The filtering arrangements created by the Bill are described in more detail in the Explanatory Notes for clauses 14-16.

33. The identity of the public authority which will assume responsibility for operating the filtering arrangements in the long term has yet to be determined. The powers in clause 20(1) and (2) accordingly cater for the possibility that the functions of the Secretary of State under clauses 14 to 16 may, at some point in the future, be transferred to another public authority designated by order, or that a public authority may carry out agency arrangements with the Secretary of State in relation to other matters falling within Part 2. The clause 20(1) power may, if necessary, be used to amend the constitution of the public authority to enable it to exercise the functions concerned. The power in clause 20(2) will enable statutory bars to be removed from public authorities acting as agents for the Secretary of State in relation to functions exercisable under Part 2. These powers will ensure that the Department retains the flexibility to determine which body is best placed to operate the arrangements or undertake other agency functions in relation to Part 2, taking into account any relevant considerations which may from time to time arise.

34. Given that the Bill vests these functions in the Secretary of State and the expected level of public interest in the operation of these arrangements, the Government considers that any transfer of functions

should be subject to prior parliamentary scrutiny and approval through the affirmative procedure (which applies by virtue of clause 29(2)(a)).

Clause 21(1) – definition of "designated senior officers": Power to specify required minimum rank, office or position.

Power conferred on: *Secretary of State*

Power exercisable by: *Order made by statutory instrument*

Parliamentary procedure: *Negative resolution*

35. Subsection (1) of clause 21 provides that "designated senior officers" means individuals holding such ranks, offices or positions with relevant public authorities as are specified by order of the Secretary of State. The designated senior officer of a relevant public authority is empowered to grant authorisations to obtain communications data under clause 9.

36. Given the number of relevant public authorities who may be designated by order it would not be practicable for the designated senior officer in respect of each public authority to be specified on the face of the legislation. Similar provision is contained in section 25(2) of RIPA (see S.I. 2010/480). The negative resolution procedure (see clause 29(3)(b)) provides the appropriate level of parliamentary scrutiny for a power of this nature.

Clause 21: Relevant public authorities –

   i.   **Subsection (1), paragraph (e) of definition of "relevant public authority": Power to add to the list of public authorities able to access communications data.**
  ii.   **Subsection (7) – Power to remove bodies from the list of public authorities able to access communications data.**
 iii.   **Subsection (8) – Power to amend enactments consequential upon a person ceasing to be a relevant public authority.**

Power conferred on: *Secretary of State*

Power exercisable by: *Order made by statutory instrument*

Parliamentary procedure: *Affirmative resolution where designating a person under paragraph (e) of definition of relevant public authority or amending or repealing primary legislation, otherwise negative resolution.*

37. Clause 21(1) (in the definition of "relevant public authority"), (7) and (8) permit the Secretary of State, by order, to designate relevant public authorities, remove public authorities from the list of relevant public authorities on the face of the Bill and to make amendments consequential on a public authority ceasing to be a relevant public authority. The powers in clause 21(1), (7) and (8) mirror those in section 25 of RIPA and have been used to add a number of public authorities to the list of relevant public authorities in Chapter 2 of Part 1 of RIPA (see S.I. 2010/480).

38. It is envisaged that the powers in subsections (1), (7) and (8) will most commonly be used to address changes to the list of relevant public authorities consequent on the abolition of a body, or the transfer of its functions to a successor body. However, the power may also be used to designate new bodies as relevant public authorities. When a new body is created by statute, for example, the need for the body to acquire communications data to carry out its functions can be overlooked. Similarly, circumstances may change over time such that an existing body may be able to present a compelling case for designation. The power in subsection (1) will ensure that public authorities obtain the communications data they need to carry out their functions in accordance with a statutory framework which provides the safeguards considered necessary by Parliament to ensure that investigatory powers are exercised compatibly with the ECHR.

39. The designation of a new body under paragraph (e) of the definition of "relevant public authority", and any amendments to primary legislation consequent on the exercise of the power, are both significant matters. Accordingly, the affirmative procedure (see clause 29(2)(b)) is considered appropriate to enable these matters to be debated in both Houses, and to ensure that the powers are subject to proper oversight and control. The negative resolution procedure is considered sufficient for any order which does not contain such provision.

Schedule 1, paragraph 4: Power to make a transfer scheme.

Power conferred on:	*Secretary of State*
Power exercisable by:	*Statutory scheme*
Parliamentary procedure:	*Affirmative resolution where included in a clause 20(1) order otherwise laid before Parliament only*

40. Paragraph 4 of Schedule 1 confers power on the Secretary of State to make a transfer scheme in connection with an order made under clause 20(1). A transfer scheme is a scheme providing for the transfer of property, rights and liabilities (including rights and liabilities relating

to contracts of employment) from the Secretary of State to another public authority.

41. Paragraph 4(3) lists consequential, supplementary, incidental and transitional provision that may be made by a transfer scheme. These include making provision the same as or similar to the TUPE regulations (the Transfer of Undertakings (Protections of Employment) Regulations 2006 (S.I. 2006/246)).

42. The Government considers it appropriate that the details of transfers of property, rights and liabilities, which may be very complex, should be set out in a transfer scheme. There are a number of precedents for such matters to be left to secondary legislation, including in section 90(1) of the Protection of Freedoms Act 2012.

43. A transfer scheme may be included in an order made under clause 20(1) (in which case the order will be subject to the affirmative procedure) but, if not so included, must be laid before Parliament after being made. This procedure will ensure that details of the transfer scheme can be combined with an order under clause 20(1) if that is considered appropriate; but provide flexibility for a transfer scheme to be made after such an order has been made where this is considered the appropriate course of action.

Schedule 1, paragraph 5: Power to vary taxation in connection with a transfer scheme.

Power conferred on: *The Treasury*

Power exercisable by: *Order made by statutory instrument*

Parliamentary procedure: *Negative resolution*

44. Paragraph 5 of Schedule 1 confers power on the Treasury by order to make provision varying the way in which certain tax provisions apply either for anything transferred under a scheme made under paragraph 4, or anything done for the purposes of, or in relation to a transfer under such a scheme. For the purposes of this power the relevant taxes are income tax, corporation tax, capital gains tax, stamp duty, stamp duty reserve tax and stamp duty land tax.

45. This power will enable the Treasury to ensure that appropriate tax provision is made, and at the appropriate time, to ensure that a transfer does not give rise to a tax change or confer a tax advantage on either party.

46. The power under paragraph 5 is exercisable by statutory instrument subject to negative procedure in the House of Commons (see clause 29(4)). This reflects the level of Parliamentary procedure applicable to

equivalent powers in section 25 of the Public Bodies Act 2011 and section 91(1) of the Protection of Freedoms Act 2012. The order is not subject to any procedure in the House of Lords, as the House of Commons is the correct forum for the determination of matters in respect of taxation.

PART 3: SCRUTINY AND OTHER PROVISIONS

Clause 24(3): Power to amend, repeal or revoke any enactment consequential upon clause 24(2).

Power conferred on:	*Secretary of State*
Power exercisable by:	*Order made by statutory instrument*
Parliamentary procedure:	*Affirmative resolution where amending or repealing primary legislation, otherwise negative resolution*

47. Clause 24 restricts the use of general information powers by public authorities to secure the disclosure by telecommunications or postal operators of communications data without the consent of the operator. Subsection (2) applies a general formula to "general information powers", as defined in subsection (4), to prevent public authorities from using such powers to secure the disclosure by telecommunications or postal operators of communications data except where the operator has given consent or the power involves a court order or other judicial authorisation or warrant. Schedule 2 textually amends the information powers most commonly used by public authorities to obtain communications data. The effect of the amendments is to repeal those powers so far as they enable public authorities to secure the disclosure by operators of communications data without the consent of the operator.

48. Subsection (3) provides that the Secretary of State may by order amend, repeal or revoke any enactment in consequence of subsection (2). This power will enable legislation to be textually amended to restrict public authorities' powers to require disclosure of communications data, so that subsection (2) no longer needs to be relied on in relation to the amended provisions. Given the vast number of general information powers in existence it is virtually impossible to identify and amend each power. Continuing reliance on these powers following the coming into force of the Bill would defeat the purpose of clause 24 and could lead to an inconsistent approach between different operators. Subsection (3) will enable textual amendments to be made to any information powers should public authorities seek to rely on these powers despite clause 24. Subsection (3) will also address the problem of new information gathering powers which may be enacted following the coming into force of the Bill that would permit public

authorities to acquire communications data from operators in contravention of the policy underpinning clause 24. While the new power should, in principle, be caught by subsection (2), it may be preferable to use the power in subsection (3) to textually amend the offending provision to provide clarity and certainty for operators and public authorities as regards the application of the law.

49. By virtue of clause 29(2)(c), an order under subsection (3) that amends or repeals any provision of primary legislation is subject to the affirmative resolution procedure thus ensuring that orders of this nature are afforded the appropriate degree of parliamentary scrutiny. Other orders under subsection (3) are subject to the negative procedure (see clause 29(3)(b)).

Schedule 3, paragraphs 3 and 6 – new section 71(4) and 71A(4) of the Regulation of Investigatory Powers Act 2000: Power to make an order bringing into force (i) code of practice and (ii) revised code of practice.

Power conferred on: *Secretary of State*

Power exercisable by: *Order made by statutory instrument*

Parliamentary procedure: *(i) Affirmative resolution; (ii) Affirmative resolution or laying only*

50. Paragraph 2 of Schedule 3 makes consequential amendments to section 71(2) of RIPA to require codes of practice to be issued under that section in respect of the powers and duties under Parts 1 and 2 of the Bill. Codes issued under section 71 are subject to the affirmative resolution procedure.

51. Paragraph 3 of Schedule 3 amends the procedure in section 71 of RIPA for issuing codes of practice under the Act. These changes respond to concerns raised by the Joint Committee on Statutory Instruments in its 30th Report of Session 2002/2003 concerning S.I. 2003/3175 made under equivalent powers in section 103 of the Anti-terrorism Crime and Security Act 2001.

52. Paragraph 6 of Schedule 3 inserts new section 71A into RIPA. The new section is designed to simplify the procedure for revising codes of practice issued under section 71. Practical experience following the enactment of RIPA suggests that the codes of practice need to be revised on a far more regular basis than had originally been envisaged. By way of example, codes of practice which mention relevant public authorities or specify authorisation levels for particular activities quickly become out of date when bodies are abolished or merge following machinery of government and other changes. In many cases, however,

the substance of the code remains the same and does not require any significant revisions.

53. Minor and technical amendments of this nature need to be made on a yearly basis (or even more frequently) if the codes are not quickly to become out of date, and potentially misleading to practitioners and others. While more significant revisions of the whole or any part of a code issued under section 71 may require the approval of both Houses of Parliament, the affirmative resolution procedure is considered to be unduly burdensome and to provide an inappropriately rigorous level of Parliamentary scrutiny in relation to minor and technical amendments to the codes. New section 71A of RIPA accordingly provides that an order bringing a revision of a code of practice into operation may either be subject to the affirmative resolution procedure or must be laid before Parliament. In both cases, the Secretary of State must first publish the code in draft and consider any representation made about it, and must lay the modified code before Parliament together with the order to which it relates.

Clause 31(2): Power to make consequential provisions for the purposes of the Bill.

Power conferred on: *Secretary of State*

Power exercisable by: *Order made by statutory instrument*

Parliamentary procedure: *Affirmative resolution where primary legislation is amended or repealed; otherwise negative resolution*

54. Clause 31(2) confers power on the Secretary of State to make such consequential provision as he or she considers appropriate for the purposes of the Bill. The power includes a power to make transitional, transitory or saving provision, and to amend or repeal any Act or subordinate legislation (subsection (3)).

55. The powers conferred by this clause are wide but are necessary, for example, to ensure that consequential amendments can be made to the functions of a designated public authority in consequence of the exercise of the power in clause 20(1). There are various precedents for such provisions including section 173 of the Serious Organised Crime and Police Act 2005, section 51 of the Police and Justice Act 2006, section 148 of the Criminal Justice and Immigration Act 2008 and section 113 of the Protection of Freedoms Act 2012. To the extent that an order under this clause amends or repeals primary legislation, it will be subject to the affirmative resolution procedure, otherwise it will be subject to the negative resolution procedure (see clause 29(2)(c) and (3)(b)). It is submitted that this provides the appropriate level of parliamentary scrutiny for the powers conferred by this clause.

Clause 32(1): Power to make transitional, transitory or saving provisions.

Power conferred on: *Secretary of State*

Power exercisable by: *Order made by statutory instrument*

Parliamentary procedure: *None*

56. Clause 32(1) confers power on the Secretary of State to make such transitional, transitory or saving provisions as he or she considers appropriate in connection with the coming into force of the provisions in the Bill. This is a standard power to enable the changes made by the Bill to be implemented in an orderly manner. Such powers are often included as part of the power to make commencement orders (for example, section 114 of the Protection of Freedoms Act 2012) and, as such, are not subject to any Parliamentary procedure on the grounds that Parliament has already approved the principle of the provisions in the Bill by enacting them. Although drafted as a free standing power on this occasion, the same principle applies and accordingly the power is not subject to any parliamentary procedure.

Clause 32(3): Power to make transitory provisions pending Scottish police reform.

Power conferred on: *Secretary of State*

Power exercisable by: *Order made by statutory instrument*

Parliamentary procedure: *Negative resolution*

57. Clause 32(2) enables the Secretary of State, by order, to make such appropriate provision to secure that the Bill has full effect despite the coming into force of particular provisions before the coming into force of Part 1 of the Police and Fire Reform (Scotland) Bill (Scotland police reform provisions). In particular, the Secretary of State may modify references in the Bill to any person, body or other thing created by the Scottish police reform provisions.

58. The Government considers it appropriate to include this power to deal with the possibility that legislation currently before the Scottish Parliament, which will significantly amend existing police force structures in Scotland, is not in force when this Bill comes into force. The timings are not yet clear and are outwith the control of the Government. But the Bill has been drafted as if the Scottish legislation is in force. It is possible, if the timings of the Scottish legislation become clear, that this power will not be needed and may be removed by amendment before the Bill is enacted.

59. The order is subject to the negative procedure (by virtue of clause 29(3)(b)) because it is considered that the provisions which could be made concern merely technical modifications to the Bill to ensure that references to Scottish police matters are accurate.

Clause 33(2): Commencement power.

Power conferred on: *Secretary of State*

Power exercisable by: *Order made by statutory instrument*

Parliamentary Procedure: *None*

60. Subsection (2) of clause 33 contains a standard power to bring provisions of the Bill into force by commencement order. As usual with the commencement orders, they are not subject to any parliamentary procedure. Parliament has approved the principle of the provisions to be commenced by enacting them; commencement by order enables the provisions to be brought into force at a convenient time.

Home Office
June 2012